Migration and Inequality

Migration and Inequality

Mirna Safi

polity

First published in 2020 by Polity Press

Polity Press
65 Bridge Street
Cambridge CB2 1UR, UK

Polity Press
101 Station Landing
Suite 300
Medford, MA 02155, USA

ISBN-13: 978-1-5095-2210-1
ISBN-13: 978-1-5095-2211-8(pb)

A catalogue record for this book is available from the British Library.

Library of Congress Cataloging-in-Publication Data
Names: Safi, Mirna, author.
Title: Migration and inequality / Mirna Safi.
Description: Cambridge, United Kingdom ; Medford, MA : Polity, 2020. |
   Includes bibliographical references and index. | Summary: "In a world of
   increasingly heated political debates on migration, this book radically
   shifts the focus to address migration through the lens of inequality.
   Mirna Safi shows migration to be a mechanism of inequality and shows how
   studying international migration can challenge current limited,
   nationally established paradigms of social justice"-- Provided by
   publisher.
Identifiers: LCCN 2019027638 (print) | LCCN 2019027639 (ebook) | ISBN
   9781509522101 (hardcover) | ISBN 9781509522118 (paperback) | ISBN
   9781509522149 (epub)
Subjects: LCSH: Emigration and immigration--Social aspects. |
   Immigrants--Social conditions. | Social justice.
Classification: LCC JV6225 .S235 2020 (print) | LCC JV6225 (ebook) | DDC
   304.8--dc23
LC record available at https://lccn.loc.gov/2019027638
LC ebook record available at https://lccn.loc.gov/2019027639

Typeset in 11 on 13pt Sabon
by Fakenham Prepress Solutions, Fakenham, Norfolk NR21 8NL
Printed and bound in Great Britain by TJ International Limited

The publisher has used its best endeavours to ensure that the URLs for external websites referred to in this book are correct and active at the time of going to press. However, the publisher has no responsibility for the websites and can make no guarantee that a site will remain live or that the content is or will remain appropriate.

Every effort has been made to trace all copyright holders, but if any have been overlooked the publisher will be pleased to include any necessary credits in any subsequent reprint or edition.

For further information on Polity, visit our website: politybooks.com

Brief Contents

Detailed Contents

Figures & Tables

Figures

Tables

Acknowledgments

This book builds heavily on former research conducted by social science scholars, the overwhelming majority of whom I do not know personally. It also owes much to colleagues I've had the tremendous opportunity to meet, work and discuss with. As enriching exchanges with Roger Waldinger encouraged me to put my thinking all together in a book, I feel particularly indebted to him now that the book is ready. I also want to extend my sincere appreciation to Patrick Simon, who supported and improved the first intellectual steps for this book. Collaborations and exchanges with him have been deeply gratifying to me on both personal and professional grounds. Additionally, the consolidation of earlier material owes a lot to formal and informal discussions I've had from outstanding colleagues like Yann Algan, Françoise Lorcerie, Andrea Réa, Donald Tomaskovic-Devey, and Andreas Wimmer.

I am also indebted to my colleagues and friends at my center, OSC-Sciences Po. Discussions with them have certainly strengthened the book. While I feel grateful to all of them, I want to express my special thanks to Carlo Barone, Philippe Coulangeon, Emanuele Ferragina, Olivier Godechot, Haley McAvey, Ettore Recchi, and Matthew

Soener for their comments, suggestions, and encouragements. Bernard Corminboeuf helped me improve the diagrams used for this project and I am profoundly grateful to him. Finally, I've been lucky to benefit from Sciences Po and the LIEPP's financial support.

I feel endlessly grateful to my family, Pierre, Tamim, Mayad, and Liya, for their unconditional love and support.

Most of this book's thinking began to take shape during a harsh personal period that will make it always be associated with the loss of my father; I would like to dedicate it to him with infinite love and respect.

Introduction: Rethinking Migration beyond Securitarianism, Humanitarianism, and Culturalism

Despite variability in demographic, political and socioeconomic contexts, immigration has been increasingly depicted as a "social problem" in public debate across Western democracies. Cross-national population movements are most commonly presented as exogenously and illegitimately affecting the economic, political, social, and cultural stability of nation-states. In most societies, immigration is thus incessantly linked to the rise of unemployment, crime, segregation, poverty, and terrorism, and is more generally presented as undermining social cohesion.

These representations generally draw on three distinct "repertoires" that fuel similar narratives about immigration in public discourse despite some variation in their combination across countries: "securitarianism," humanitarianism and culturalism. Securitarianism denotes the increasing tendency to relate migration to the issue of security of physical borders in the nation-state. This entails the now well-established restrictive turn in immigration policy, with harsher entry rules and increasingly militarized border controls becoming a worldwide model of migration governance. Humanitarianism refers to the inclination to present migrant reception as a "humanitarian act" in wealthy and stable societies that cannot close their eyes to the political, economic, or social injustice usually depicted in the global South. Receiving migrants who seek a better life is therefore a question of generosity, and the political debate is concerned by the degree to which such an aim should and could be fulfilled, as clearly shown by the recent "refugee crisis." Finally, culturalism pertains to the tendency to perceive immigration as injecting cultural differences in receiving societies (religion, language, norms and values, ways of being, etc.). Whether politically framed as involving cultural "diversity" or cultural "fragmentation," culturalism draws on the substantive association of immigration with increasing heterogeneity in nation-states originally perceived as ethnically or culturally homogeneous. Although they may bear upon distinctive political and philosophical backgrounds, these three repertoires (securitarianism, humanitarianism, and culturalism) share the common assumption that the nation-state's perimeter naturally and legitimately limits equal access to political, economic, cultural, and symbolic resources between migrants and non-migrants. Notwithstanding the preconceptions they convey, the public debates surrounding migration are indicative of the degree to which the subject touches central social issues with implications of social justice and the distribution of economic, political, cultural, and symbolic resources.

These repertoires have impacted social science research on migration and fueled its impressive proliferation over the last several decades. Stepping back from immediate policy debates, this book offers a synthesis of this vast literature with a social stratification lens highlighting the specific channels through which migration contributes to the (re)making of inequality. Social inequality is defined in a broad sense: it refers to the fact that some individuals, families, groups, countries (or any other relevant social category) enjoy a disproportionate share of some desired good (income, wealth, rights, respect, etc.). Textbooks on inequality overwhelmingly focus on the triptych class/race/gender. Migration is sporadically tackled through its relation to class and/or race and is rarely treated as a specific component of inequality. This book presents a unified framework relating migration to social inequality. It therefore aims at bridging the gap between three relatively distinct social science fields: migration and immigration studies, ethnic and racial studies, and social stratification and inequality studies. Positioning migration research at the crossroads of these scientific streams fosters our understanding of both migratory dynamics and social inequality mechanisms.

The first chapter maps the terrain of the book. It summarizes contemporary patterns and trends in migration and discusses definition and measurement issues. It also identifies the main areas of inquiry in the field, covering a variety of disciplinary perspectives and theoretical approaches. Chapter 2 moves to the field of stratification and discusses its contemporary developments. Drawing on an analytical framework that summarizes social stratification elementary mechanisms, this chapter attempts to synthetically conceptualize the relation between migration and inequality by identifying three main channels. The next three chapters elaborate on each of these channels. Chapter 3 reviews the literature that has traditionally associated migration with the global division of labor, thus entailing the joint mechanisms of workers' categorization and redistribution of economic resources. Chapter 4 builds on insights from legal and political scholarship that insist on the way in which migration creates and reshapes inequality through the joint mechanisms of citizenship categorization and redistribution of legal resources. Chapter 5 deals with the symbolic channel through which migration impacts inequality by reconfiguring group boundary dynamics and reshaping ethnoracial classifications. Each chapter starts with an assessment of theories informing the effect of migration on inequality, before moving to the main empirical findings in the corresponding literature. The conclusion discusses current concerns about migration in the light of its conceptualization as a case-study for inequality research.

– 1 –

From National to Migration Societies

This chapter provides an overview of the demographic scope of international migration and examines the main challenges it raises in contemporary societies. First, I present the definition of international migration and introduce related concepts such as immigrant generations and immigrant origins. I then move to summarizing the long-term trends in migration flows with a particular focus on Western societies. The final section summarizes the state of the field, identifying three main directions in which migration research has been developing: the driving factors of population movements, the process of assimilation of immigrants and their descendants in host societies, and the effects of migration in sending and receiving societies.

Basic Definitions and Measurements Issues

From geographic mobility to international migration

Migration is central to human history (Fisher 2014). The concept is very broad, and it concerns each one of us to varying degrees. While some people spend most of their lives migrating (nomadic groups, seasonal workers, diplomats, travelers, etc.), moving to a new place during the life course is likely to occur at least a few times, usually in relation to individual events, such as unions, family separation and re-composition, childbearing and job seeking; or collective ones, such as wars, revolutions, famines, natural disasters, etc. Major historical processes such as conquests and military conflicts, slavery, empire building, colonization and decolonization, urbanization and environmental change have all occurred in relation to intense population movements. So have most technological advancements and innovations, like hunting, sailing, agriculture, industrialization, etc.

A definition of migration that encompasses the wide diversity of migratory patterns emphasizes the "cross-community movement" that it entails (Manning 2013).[1] While spatial mobility can be fundamentally understood as core human behavior, the scope and delimitation of human communities have continually changed over history, which in turn has affected the definition of human migration. Languages have been a central marker of community boundaries, and processes of differentiation and convergence of languages have been closely related to human movements across the globe; along with genetics, linguistic evidence is the most commonly used indicator for inferring ancient patterns of migration. The focus of this book is on a particular type of "modern migration," which can be called "cross-political-community migration" in a context where all the earth's land has been virtually claimed by fewer than 200 globally recognized national entities.[2] It is this particular type of modern geographic mobility, referred to as *international migration*, that will be most relevant in the following pages. Much like the evolution of language boundaries, nation-building processes have been intertwined with human migration and continue to be affected by it.

In parallel to international migration, internal migration constitutes a considerable share of overall human migration.[3] Sometimes referred to as residential mobility, it is a major phenomenon in large countries such as India and China. Despite occurring within nation-states, internal migration sometimes entails the crossing of administrative and political boundaries (states, regions, provinces, etc.). Although I do not elaborate in this book on internal migration, we should bear in mind that its relationship to labor and to its socio-legal status, as well as its effects on group boundary-making, share many aspects with international migration.

Who counts as a migrant? An ascriptive, durable, and transmissible status

When I discuss the definition of international migration with students, it is not unusual to notice that some of them are quite surprised, if not troubled, when they realize that they may fit the description. One of them once told me: "According to your definition, I would be an immigrant. There is something wrong there." The student in question was born in Egypt and lived there for only a few years, during which time his parents were working there. His family, of relatively high socioeconomic background, moved back to France, where he grew up, went to school, and attended college. The word "immigrant" was obviously negatively charged for him, and his reaction was to challenge any identification of his personal experience with the subject matter of the course.

Migrants are among the most stigmatized population categories in Western democracies. Social representations spread by the media and political debates tend to draw strong associations with the undocumented, the poor, the minorities, etc. Western workers who settle in developing countries are rarely referred to as immigrants – they are most often called "expats." And this is true even within developed countries: immigrants in France are rarely portrayed as Germans or Swiss, for example, even though these countries are the birthplaces of a considerable share of French residents and are included in immigration national statistics. The use of words such as migrant or immigrant in the public debate conveys a variety of connotations (socioeconomic, ethnoracial, legal, etc.), thus diverging from its scientific definition. But how then do we define international migrants?

One needs to migrate to be a migrant, and migration is a movement in place between two observational moments. The very concept of migration consequently requires delimiting boundaries of space and time. As mentioned above, international migration is usually defined by relying on national categorization of space: international migrants move across national boundaries. The definition also uses birth date as a time reference: international migrants move away from their country of birth.[4]

When one considers a given country c at a given time t, it thus becomes possible to define the immigrant population as being composed of persons who live in c at time t even though they were born in another country (c').[5] This population is also referred to as "foreign-born." Relying on this definition, the international migrant population can be estimated worldwide: in 2015, the number of immigrants stood at almost 244 million, according to the UN Population Division; this means that about 3.3 percent of the earth's inhabitants currently live in a country different from their country of birth. A major share of current migration moves to the "developed countries"; 23 percent of migrants actually migrate within the Northern part of the globe, and 35 percent take the South–North migration path. South–South migration remains nonetheless considerable (around 35 percent of worldwide international migration). Top sending countries are India (15.6 million), Mexico (12.3 million), Russia (10.6 million) and China (9.5 million), while top receiving countries are the United States (46.6 million), Germany (12 million), Russia (11.6 million) and Saudi Arabia (10.2 million). In relative terms, the proportion of the foreign-born exceeds 80 percent in several Persian Gulf countries, such as the United Arab Emirates and Qatar. This share is around 13 percent in OECD countries, exceeding 25 percent in countries such as Luxembourg, Switzerland,

and Australia, while countries such as the United States, the United Kingdom, Germany, and France are closer to the OECD average (see Figure 1.1 for more details).

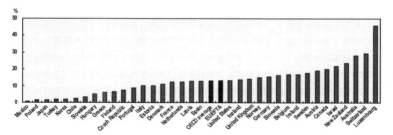

Figure 1.1 The foreign-born as a percentage of the total population in OECD countries, 2017
Source: OECD International Migration Database

Since it is closely linked to the delimitation of national boundaries, the definition of migration is subject to political disputation. An instructive example can be found in the definition of "immigrant" in postcolonial contexts. In France, for instance, the "foreign-born" definition has been considered unsatisfactory, since it includes French return colonials ("repatriates") and French emigrants' children born abroad.[6] France's public statistics institutions thus prefer a more complex definition, adding a nationality-at-birth criterion: an immigrant is a person who was born abroad and is non-French at birth. This two-criteria definition is intrinsically political, since both categories are, strictly speaking, migrants: they moved away from their place of birth and across national borders (Beauchemin and Safi 2019). Yet their migration is not considered to have crossed the "political community" borders, either because the geographic borders themselves moved in the meantime (in the case of return colonials), or because transmitting political membership (nationality) is made possible beyond the geographic limits of the state (in the case of emigrants' children). The decision to exclude

them from the immigrant population is also justified by the
fact that the social trajectories of these populations, who
were recognized as French citizens at birth, sharply differ
from those of other foreign-born populations (on political,
socioeconomic, linguistic, cultural, and symbolic grounds).

This example clearly shows that while the definition
of international migration derives from a country-level
classification, it also relates to the concept of "society,"
thus involving a combination of geographic, political,
social, cultural, and symbolic dimensions. Other examples
can be found in complex migration settings such as
return colonial migration from South Africa to the United
Kingdom, national overseas migrants in France, internal
rural migrants in China, Puerto Rican migrants in the
United States, etc. International statistics on migration
tend to overlook these specific cases, using the foreign-born
definition as an operational one in comparative perspective.

From the point of view of the receiving country, one
important implication of the definition of international
migration lies in the fact that, as long as settlement endures,
immigrants remain immigrants: one can therefore speak of
immigrant status as a stable one in host societies. It may
also be regarded as an ascriptive status[7] since it is linked to
a place of birth criterion, which renders it a characteristic
that individuals cannot alter (Shachar 2009).[8] Here it is
important to distinguish the concept of immigrant from
the neighboring concept of foreigner: while foreigners can
acquire citizenship and thus become nationals – more or
less easily, depending on the host country's citizenship legislation – it is only when immigrants reto live in their country
of birth that they stop being immigrants.[9] In other words,
immigrants remain immigrants even when they acquire their
host country's citizenship. Moreover, the immigrant status
itself tends to be transmissible. Indeed, debates on migration
often go beyond the experience of migrants themselves to
encompass that of their offspring, usually referred to as
second-generation immigrants. Even when born in the host
country – which means that they did not experience migration

– and even when the host country grants them nationality (by birth or in early age stages), immigrant descendants are still part of the immigration debate both in the academic and the political sphere (Luthra et al. 2018). Moreover, the distinction between first- and second-generation immigrants is not as clear-cut as it may appear: immigrant descendants who were born in the origin country and migrated with their parents when young are, strictly speaking, immigrants themselves (since they live in a country different from their country of birth). One may nonetheless argue that they are quite similar to native-born second-generation immigrants. Moreover, some immigrant descendants have a mixed background if they have one native parent, which may render their social experience quite different. This led some scholars to argue in favor of a finer classification of immigrant generations, such as the decimal system intro-duced by Rumbaut (2004). Among the first generation, this classification distinguishes between earlier arrived migrants (G1.5) and migrants arrived as adults (G1). Among migrant descendants, researchers usually distinguish between mixed-ascendance second generations (G2.5) and children of two immigrant parents (G2). All in all, migration scholars and statistical agencies have been using information on nativity, parental nativity, and sometimes age at migration to produce a number of different generational classifications of immigrants. As discussed in the following section, these debates on immigrant generations are closely related to the assimilation paradigm. At this stage, it is worth highlighting that, from the perspective of the receiving country, *the immigrant definition entails an ascriptive, durable and somehow transmissible status*. As discussed in the rest of the book, this has major implications on the dynamics of social inequality in supposedly meritocratic societies that receive a considerable share of international migrants.

In most countries, people tend to overestimate the immigrant population (Alba et al. 2005; Herda 2010; Hainmueller and Hopkins 2014). This is undoubtedly related to the increasing salience of immigration in the political debate, most often portrayed as an uncontrolled invasion. But this overestimation might also be related to the intrinsic fuzziness of the concept, as discussed above; distinctions of immigrant cohorts and generations, heterogeneity in terms of countries of origin and socioeconomic status also contribute to blurring the boundaries between immigrant and non-immigrant populations in social representations (see Table 1.1).

Table 1.1   Perceived and real proportion of the foreign-born population in some OECD countries (%)

	Perceived proportion of immigrants, 2014	Real proportion of immigrants, 2014
Austria	26.2	16.59
Belgium	29.1	15.64
Switzerland	31.3	26.82
Czech Republic	9.1	3.77
Germany	22.4	12.14
Denmark	13.6	10.12
Estonia	21.6	14.94
Spain	21.8	12.81
Finland	9.5	5.46
France	26.0	11.72
UK	27.3	12.50
Hungary	11.2	4.53
Ireland	20.1	16.10
Lithuania	11.2	4.67
Netherlands	23.8	11.61
Norway	16.2	13.79
Poland	9.1	1.63
Portugal	24.1	8.24
Sweden	20.6	15.89
Slovenia	23.2	11.42

Source: Perceived proportion: European Social Survey, round 7, 2014 (https://www.europeansocialsurvey.org/data/download.html?r=7); real proportion: Eurostat 2014 (http://appsso.eurostat.ec.europa.eu/nui/show.do?dataset=migr_imm8&lang=en)

Patterns and Trends in International Migration: A Brief History

Is international migration on the rise? The value of long-term perspectives

Quantifying the long-term evolution of human migration is a complex task. Vast transformations of structural conditions have affected the quantity of flows and their routes; while, in the past, travelers used their feet, horses, or boats to move across the globe, the accumulation of existing linkages and connections created by former flows, along with technological advancement in transportation and communication, has opened new routes for human mobility. Moreover, and conversely to the relative stability of natural geography, the boundaries that are relevant to measuring migration – in other words, human geography – have kept changing. The most recent decades witnessed huge transformations in the institutional governance of migration driven by the generalization of restrictive policies, tougher and increasingly sophisticated border control and hardening anti-immigration attitudes. These transformations limit the scope of comparisons in the long run.

Historical perspectives remain useful nonetheless, mainly because they challenge some misconceptions on the exceptional nature of current migration. Far from being a characteristic feature of the present era, migratory flows have been constantly reshaping the world population distribution through small-scale yet steady population movements. Historians thus tend to see migration as a slow and self-sustaining process that keeps changing the face of the world. They also agree on the fact that the period from 1850 to 1930 was the most intensive era of migration in human history (Manning 2013: 154). This age of mass migration witnessed the journey of more than 60 million Europeans moving to the four corners of the earth, settling in the Americas, Australia, New Zealand, and South Africa (Hatton and Williamson 1998). Migration at the turn of the twentieth century consequently led to a reallocation of the earth's inhabitants across the continents, with huge and ongoing effects on languages, cultures, and economic dynamics. The post-World War II period was also marked by massive episodes of migration. Long-distance movements after 1945 involved all regions of the world, with greater mobility from Asia, Africa, and Latin America.

Regarding the most recent period, finer data allow even more precise analyses. An extensive worldwide database has been built by the World Bank, compiling more than a thousand national censuses and population registers. Using this data, Özden and coauthors (2011) sketch a global origin-destination migration matrix for each decade in the period between 1960 and 2000. Their research shows that, while there is indeed an increase in absolute value, global migration as a percentage of the worldwide population actually tends to decrease (2011: 3). The authors also find evidence of spread in the scope of migration and multiplication of migration corridors, which they interpret as growing connectedness between countries in terms of bilateral migration. Using the same data, Czaika and De Haas (2014) argue that most general assumptions do not hold on the global level: neither the increasing trends, nor diversification, nor extension of geographic scope, nor even feminization. The authors particularly emphasize variability in the conclusions that one may draw, depending on the perspectives of sending or receiving societies. While emigrants tend to come from increasingly diversified countries, they are concentrating more and more in a few destination countries (the United States, Canada, Australia, Germany, the Gulf countries). This shift in the global directionality of migration is mainly driven by the transformation of Europe from a global source region of emigrants and settlers into a global migration magnet. The fact that national and ethnic origins of the immigrant population have become increasingly non-European might be lying behind a Eurocentric vision of migration as a growing phenomenon. The data used by Özden et al. and by Czaika and De Haas only goes as far as 2000; more recent data on worldwide migration nonetheless confirms that the increase in international migration remains modest in proportional terms (2.8 percent of the world population in 2000 to 3.3 percent in 2015) (IOM 2017: 15).

Are we experiencing a "migrant crisis"?

With migration currently in the spotlight, it has become common to read and hear that the world is experiencing a "crisis," especially since 2015. It is alternately referred to as a "migrant crisis" and a "refugee crisis," with increasingly politicized distinctions between the two expressions.[10] Despite being perceptible in the United States, Canada and other central immigration countries, this discourse is the most powerful in Europe, marked by a tangible rise in refugee flows and asylum requests in recent years. Violent conflicts in Syria, Iraq, and other Middle Eastern and African countries have been displacing masses, mostly to poor and middle-income neighboring countries, but also to a lesser extent to Europe, mainly via Greece, Bulgaria, Italy, Spain, Malta, and Cyprus. More than a million people crossed into Europe in 2015, and similar figures have been estimated for 2016. Within Europe, the overwhelming majority of refugees have been hosted by Germany and Sweden. In early 2017, the number of refugees in the world exceeded 22 million, while the number of displaced (including within nation-states) was around 65 million.

There is an ongoing debate on the extent to which the current migrant crisis deserves this denomination (Dustmann et al. 2016; Hatton 2016; Holmes and Castañeda 2016). As mentioned above, historical research shows that long-distance geographic mobility is not quantitatively more intense today; current migration flows indeed lag behind the ones experienced during the age of "mass migration" at the turn of the twentieth century and post-1945 migration. And even if the comparison were to be limited to refugee flows, the current events are not so exceptional: around 18 million refugees fled Southeastern Europe after the fall of the Berlin wall and the dissolution of Yugoslavia; most of them sought asylum in European states. Consequently, quantitatively speaking, qualifying the current period as a migratory crisis does not seem to be appropriate. And in any case, if a crisis does exist, it is not OECD countries but developing, conflict-neighboring countries such as Turkey, Lebanon, and Jordan that have been carrying out the bulk of it (see Figure 1.2).[11] Figure 1.3 shows that the "humanitarian" type of migration has remained a small share of overall migration flows to OECD countries during the last decade.

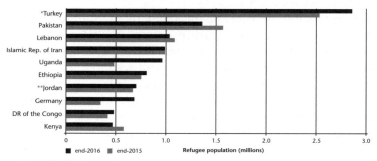

* Refugee figure for Syrians in Turkey was a government estimate.
** Includes 33,100 Iraqi refugees registered with UNHCR in Jordan. The government estimated the number of Iraqis at 400,000 individuals at the end of March 2015. This includes refugees and other categories of Iraqis.

Figure 1.2 Major refugee hosting countries in 2015 and 2016
Source: UNHCR 2017: 15

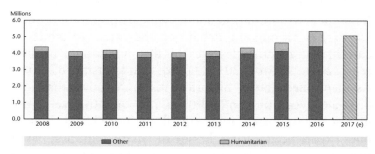

Figure 1.3 The share of humanitarian migration in overall permanent migration flows to OECD countries, 2008–2017
Source: OECD calculations based on national statistics: http://dx.doi.org/10.1787/888933750947

The global context of migration has nonetheless changed, which may explain why it is increasingly perceived as a crisis. First, the hegemonic organization of the world into nation-states undoubtedly created increasing political pressure on migration. While migration flows at the turn of the twentieth century were mostly spontaneous and unregulated, and those of the post-1945 period were mostly commanded by the hosting countries themselves, today's migration poses increasing challenges to the nation-state and questions its ability to regulate movements of people across its boundaries (Hollifield 2006; Brubaker 2010). This feeds a certain lack of confidence in the capacity of political leaders to manage the phenomenon and reach viable and acceptable solutions (Banulescu-Bogdan and Papademetriou 2016). Thus, the migrant crisis is also one of political governance and trust, at the level both of the European institutions and of individual member states.

But recent migration is not only a question of border control. Migration is increasingly experienced and represented in terms of a "crisis" because it provokes clear hostility within receiving societies, exacerbating xenophobic and racial tensions in the political debate. Images of brutality against migrants crossing the borders of Eastern Europe are extreme illustrations of this deep discomfort. The increasing political salience of immigration is reflected in the rise of xenophobic sentiment and the expanding influence of the far right in many countries. As recently shown in the United Kingdom and the United States, attitudes toward immigration have been particularly influential in orienting the political debate, directly affecting election results. Social sciences still poorly understand the channels through which these attitudes take shape and how they evolve. In many countries, recent studies have been suggesting a hiatus between people's representations toward migration and its underlying demographic and socioeconomic realities (Dustmann and Preston 2007; Hopkins et al. 2016; Sides 2016). Empirical assessments have increasingly been challenging established theories on the topic, such as minority threat and economic competition (Hainmueller and Hopkins 2014); they suggest that attitudes toward immigration are largely symbolic in nature and that emotions, moral commitments and salience in the public sphere play an important role in shaping the collective ethos related to the topic (Dustmann and Preston 2007; Sides and Citrin 2007; Merolla et al. 2013). Evidence also points to the role of political leadership and media coverage in creating and sustaining a spillover of misconceptions and beliefs that become increasingly disconnected from facts and realities (Berry et al. 2016). The proliferation of information and its increasingly unregulated and uncontrolled nature within formal and informal media are making evidence-based discourse all the less audible. Moreover, the current immigration political debate is highly sensitive toward, and overlaps with, other issues such as international conflicts and terrorism, as well as narratives about crime, ethnoracial and religious diversity, gender politics, and other highly influential public topics.

Finally, current migration is described as a crisis because it poses, more explicitly than previously, moral dilemmas in societies that hold up democracy, individual freedom, and human equality as core values. Within a context where restrictive migration policy has been prevailing in most European countries, current migration is overwhelmingly related to violent conflicts involving refugee flows characterized by intense psychological and physical despair as well as tragic deaths widely covered by the media. In 2016, the European Commission referred to it as the "largest global humanitarian crisis of our time." The photo of the Syrian toddler (Aylan), who drowned while attempting to cross the Mediterranean with his family in September 2015, provoked intense shock and quickly circulated around the world. In 2015, 3,777 deaths in the Mediterranean were recorded, and 5,079 in 2016. The crisis thus highlights issues of worldwide inequality in opportunity, status, and rights, challenging the morality of the current asylum system and beyond, the sustainability of huge between-country inequality. While far from being rare, shows of generosity and warm welcomes in some countries and regions contrast with the dominant anti-immigration discourse, highlighting the moral concerns underlying current migration.

Migration Studies in the Social Sciences: An Overview

Driven by distinct disciplinary perspectives and a variety of theoretical and empirical backgrounds, social scientists have been tackling international migration across a wide range of research questions. This section summarizes the state of the field, identifying three main directions in which migration research has been developing: the driving factors of population movements, the process of assimilation of immigrants and their descendants, and the consequences of immigration on sending and receiving societies.

Why do people move? Theories of migration

Migration studies have been primarily concerned with explaining population movements. In the late nineteenth century, Ernst Georg Ravenstein (1885, 1889), a German-English geographer and cartographer, highlighted some stylized facts associated with human migration. He particularly emphasized the self-sustaining nature of human migration flows, the role of families and networks, and the link between migration and urbanization. These "laws of migration" were reinterpreted in the neoclassical theory as a combination of push and pull factors (Lee 1966). These seminal intuitions paved the way for the development of migration theory within a broad and interdisciplinary research field. The formation of migration intentions has been shown to be driven by complex processes with multiple interconnections between micro, meso, and macro conditions leading to "cumulative causation" (Massey et al. 1993; Massey 1999; Piché 2013). Micro-level perspectives, particularly popular among economists, usually consider human capital to be the main factor affecting the migratory decision. This approach highlights individual cost/benefit considerations studied in relation to differentials in wages, skills returns, access to public goods, welfare and taxation, and other economic gains (Sjaastad 1962; Clark et al. 2007). Some social psychological research also emphasizes the importance of personality traits and personal biography (Berry 2001; Boneva and Frieze 2001).

On the meso level, factoring in the role of the household in the migration decision was proven to be crucial. Family members' migration can indeed be understood as a strategy of risk minimization and diversification of income sources (Stark and Bloom 1985; Stark 1991). The household approach reveals the variations in the reasons for mobility by gender and family status and the differential impact of migration on men and women, which significantly improves our understanding of the causes of migration (Cerrutti and Massey 2001; Curran and Rivero-Fuentes 2003). Beyond the household, the meso level more generally emphasizes the role of networks in creating durable and self-sustaining chain migration between sending and receiving societies.

Macro perspectives, on the other hand, stress global income distribution, differential population growth, globalization, wars, conflicts, and environmental risks as decisive determinants of human migration. Following a sort of "gravity model," migration is also shown to decrease with geographic distance between countries; it is also significantly higher between country pairs that share a land border, a common language, and historical colonial linkages (Mayda 2010). Within the macro-level factors, political approaches more specifically put forward the role of the nation-state building process. The implementation of state-level management of human mobility highlights the social construction of modern international migration. As territorial, cultural, and political boundaries do not always coincide in nation-state formation, state transformation dynamics thus become major determinants of human flows, sometimes taking the shape of forced migration and refugee movements (powerful examples may be found in the Armenian migration at the turn of the twentieth century and the post-Yugoslavian migration in the early 1990s). In brief, human movement is closely related to the movement of the nation-state's borders themselves (Hein 1993).

All in all, these multilevel research perspectives provide a complex theory of migration in which economic, social, cultural, political, and environmental factors interact. While not always explicitly factored in, social inequalities definitely play a role in shaping migration (Faist 2016). The most overt associations can be found in the global inequality research field: using globally harmonized data, Milanovic (2016) shows that 60 percent of individual income indeed depends on country of birth. Between-country inequality thus leads to a "citizenship rent" (or citizenship penalty) conducive to population movements. Simulations eliminating barriers to migration predict that half the population of non-OECD countries would emigrate, thus increasing global economic well-being through redistributive effects (Clemens 2011). While these estimations might appear unrealistic in the near future, direct questions on intentions to migrate do show that current migration is generally smaller than potential flows; the latest estimations of Gallup surveys find that 14 percent of the world's adults express a desire to migrate, if they had the opportunity to do so.

Other economic perspectives compare levels of inequality in origin and host countries. In his seminal work, Borjas (1987; 1994) predicts negative selection if the latter is less unequal. While evidence of negative selectivity in the United States is mixed, the European context invalidates the theory with more overt evidence of positive selection. Differentials in returns to skills and poverty constraints are shown to be decisive in the selectivity of migrants (Grogger and Hanson 2011; Belot and Hatton 2012).

Conversely, some studies stress that it is the level of inequality within the origin country that drives migration independently from the host country (Stark 2006). This is corroborated by Liebig and Sousa-Poza's (2004) large-scale comparative study covering 23 countries, which uses a question on the will to move to another country to improve work or living conditions in the 1995 International Social Survey Program. The authors show that the Gini coefficient in the origin country has a significantly positive impact on the propensity to migrate. Finally, and beyond economic considerations, environmental and political migrations may also be understood to be a reaction to other forms of inequality related to uneven access to natural resources, peace, security, and democracy. In a recent empirical assessment, Clemens (2017) shows that violence may be at least as powerful as economics in driving human migration.

What do migrants become? Theories of assimilation and integration

Initially forged by the seminal sociological tradition of the Chicago School, the concept of immigrant assimilation/ integration has been exported across national settings, disciplinary boundaries, and theoretical strands. Studies on immigrant assimilation represent the vast majority of research on migration, whether they deal with labor market incorporation, housing and spatial outcomes, educational achievement, health and well-being, values, lifestyles, religion, identity, political incorporation and voting, unions and family formation, cultural practices, etc. While the term "assimilation" remains predominant in the US literature, the term "integration" has prevailed in Europe over the last decades. It is much more commonly used by international organizations such as the OECD and the European Commission in their attempts to implement comparative indicators (OECD 2012; EU

2013). Assimilation is sometimes considered to suffer from heavier normative connotation. The legacy of French colonial assimilationism has, for example, led to the quasi-banning of the term in the public debate, which is also the case in many European countries. In Canada, it is not unusual to use words such as integration, adaptation, or accommodation rather than assimilation. In US sociology, even if assimilation is still used, its underlying conceptions and mechanisms have been intensely reassessed through vehement theoretical and empirical controversies throughout the twentieth century. Thus, one might argue that the distinction between assimilation and integration is largely a matter of rhetoric. In the most general sense, both words refer to a broad process that describes the "fate" of immigrants in host societies. In the earlier work of sociologists, this fate was supposed to follow a somehow deterministic course, a sort of "natural process." Highly influenced by the functionalism of the pioneer European sociologists, the Chicago School theorized a cycle of "race relations" that would ultimately lead immigrants to blend and assimilate in the mainstream.[12] From this perspective, immigration became a fundamental topic in American sociology, one that exemplified the power of "socialization," a concept that has been at the foundation of the discipline. Migration provokes a shock of socialization, theorized as a sort of disruptive effect; it becomes a factor of anomie (or disconnection within the social system), potentially carrying with it "dysfunctions" such as loss of references, psychological suffering, deviance, insecurity, etc. This break-up is nonetheless compensated by a process of re-socialization – and that is precisely what assimilation refers to – which links these individuals back to the social system. The most emblematic Chicagoan assimilation mechanism is that of acculturation. Acculturation entails de-socialization followed by re-socialization; the migrant, portrayed as a "marginal man" (Park 1928), progressively detaches himself from his culture of origin to embrace that of the host society. This painful process of de-socialization/re-socialization takes place over time and across generations; it is conceived of as the driver of assimilation. The passage from the first to the second generation consequently leads to increasing economic, social, and political incorporation in the host society. The concept of immigrant generations may be seen in this regard in close relation to a time-driven theorization of the assimilation process that almost works as an "invisible hand."[13]

Inherited from the earliest work of sociologists, this conceptualization has been subjected to severe criticism. The Chicago School sense of assimilation – also called "straight line assimilation" – has been accused of being "individualistic," "assimilationist," and even "ethnocentric." It has also been decried as insufficiently valid, empirically speaking. American sociologists actively engaged in deconstructing the concept all through the second half of the twentieth century, pointing out its major "anomalies" (Zhou 1997) to such an extent that some scholars raised the question of the possible "death of assimilation" (Glazer 1993). Criticism mainly pertained to the consistency and the homogeneity of the process, instead highlighting distinct and more or less independent dimensions. Gordon (1964) identified seven "assimilation stages," and Gans (1997) emphasized the difference between cultural and structural assimilation. Portes and colleagues deconstructed the process into three ideal-typical "modes of incorporation" depending on the combination of the roles of individuals, communities, and contexts of reception. Their segmented assimilation theory even predicts potential "downward assimilation" for immigrant descendants of low social capital groups that are severely discriminated against (Portes and Zhou 1993; Portes and Rumbaut 2001). Finally, since the 1990s, the transnational perspective in immigration studies has developed within a critical stance vis-à-vis conventional approaches of assimilation. Glick Schiller and colleagues' earliest work (1992) exalted the upheaval of a new class of "transmigrants" whose lives are spread across nation-state borders through all kinds of connections (social contacts, economic transfers, multiple identities, etc.). Original formulations of the transnational paradigm argue that the assimilation-oriented literature fails to capture the part of the immigrant trajectory that takes place in the country of origin, or in relation with the country of origin. Sustained transnational relations over time and across immigrant generations are thus presented as an alternative to the straight-line assimilation trajectory, suggesting that some aspects of durable linkages to the country of origin are actually consistent with "successful" incorporation into the host country (Portes et al. 1999).[14]

In their book *Remaking the American Mainstream* (2003), currently one of the most cited in the field, Alba and Nee acknowledge most of the criticism that was formulated throughout the second half of the twentieth century. They construct analytic bridges that relate immigration theory to the field of ethnicity and race more explicitly than ever before. Drawing on the constructivist perspective of group boundary-making, their "rehabilitated" theory of assimilation thus becomes centered on the dynamics of ethnoracial boundaries in a context of migration; some migrants manage to cross group boundaries individually (with the help of human capital, intermarriage, social mobility, etc.), while others need collective forms of *boundary shifting* in order to experience social mobility (for example, Irish migration in the United States). Alba and Nee argue that the Chicago model of assimilation corresponds to a dynamic of the type of *boundary blurring* that leads to the attenuation of group distinctions over time and across generations. These boundary movements and transformations are heavily affected by structural factors (namely demographic, institutional, and labor market contexts). Strongly inspired by the work of Shibutani and Kwan (1965) and their concept of "ethnic stratification," Alba and Nee's analysis of immigrant assimilation is impregnated with stratificationist flavor and more overtly related to inequality (or achieving equality in host societies) in socioeconomic, cultural, and symbolic terms. Their rehabilitation of assimilation also comes hand in hand with its conception as a two-way and even a multi-way process that involves not only changes in trajectories of migrants themselves but also in the evolution of the host society (Garcés-Mascareñas and Penninx 2015).

It is nonetheless significant that most empirical studies that adopt the perspective of assimilation (which basically consists of comparing immigrants' and their descendants' outcomes in diverse social spheres to those of non-immigrants) find a wide heterogeneity of immigrant trajectories across groups (Heath and Cheung 2007; Alba and Foner 2016; Luthra et al. 2018). Group-level disparities are overwhelmingly measured across national, ethnic, or racial lines with some additional variations along gender and generations. When explaining group-differences in "integration outcomes" such as educational achievement, urban segregation, labor market attainment, intermarriage, political incorporation, etc., interpretations draw on cultural distance and ethnic retention, on the one hand, and/or discrimination and structural barriers, on the other, as major explanatory factors. The observation of persisting gaps over the generations put into perspective the analytical power of the concept of immigrant generation, largely conceptualized in a deterministic (quasi-biological) fashion rooted in the earlier assimilationist visions (Sayad 1994; Eckstein 2002). While all second generations do have a migratory background in common, there is now a general consensus in the literature on the fact that they do not follow a single trajectory. Other lines of division (socio-legal status, socioeconomic status, context of reception, ethnoracial background, etc.) overlap with generational distinctions, blurring the uniformity of the intergenerational trend (Portes and Rumbaut 2001; Waters and Jiménez 2005; Alba and Waters 2011; McAvay 2018; Safi 2018). The conceptualization of immigrant generation as "a lineal process" (Levitt and Jaworsky 2007: 133) is all the more questionable in host societies where immigration has been continuously diffusing, thus creating "immigrant replenishment" and "complex ethnicity" (Massey 1995; Jiménez 2008).

All in all, and despite the many criticisms that the classical conception of assimilation has undergone in recent decades and the various attempts to rehabilitate it, its widespread use in the scientific and public spheres continues to be instilled with its original conceptualization in terms of convergence. In that respect, assimilation approaches a sort of "benign narrative" that is emblematic of the earliest sociological theories, considering that the history of modern societies is moving toward a reduction of social inequalities (Grusky and Ku 2008). Contemporary concerns conversely emphasize the mechanisms generating and reproducing social inequalities in the trajectories of migrants and their descendants. While not denying the fact that several forms of assimilation do occur in the long run, these perspectives depart from its conception as a "catch-up" process leading to equalization between immigrants and natives over time and across generations.

What are the consequences of migration?

Human migration engenders a myriad of consequences: demographic (population growth, aging, fertility rates, population re-composition, etc.), economic (growth, development, wages, unemployment, welfare provisions, etc.), social (social cohesion and conflict, segregation, discrimination, education, crime, etc.), political (citizenship rights, political representativeness, political polarization, multicultural policy, etc.) and cultural (cultural blending in art, music, lifestyles, cuisine, etc.). Covering all these dimensions is beyond the scope of this book. I focus here on addressing the major research questions that relate migration consequence to issues of social inequalities.

One may first consider the benefits and costs of migration for migrants themselves. Research investigating this question is mainly concerned with whether migration does improve the fate of migrants in line with what the neoclassical approach tends to expect. Most studies focus on how migrants compare to their home country population (Borjas et al. 1992; Ottaviano and Peri 2008). Data that account for income and standard of living conditions tend to confirm the individual benefits of migration (Axelsson and Westerlund 1998), although there is evidence that these migration returns vary considerably alongside characteristics such as gender, education, prior labor market experience, country of origin, etc. Borjas and coauthors (1992) find that migrants' economic trajectories may start with a relative loss in earnings followed by eventual gains depending on labor market integration. Causal evidence nonetheless remains scarce, mainly because of a lack of data that cover both pre- and post-migration individual trajectories and also because of confounding effects of selection on migration-related outcomes (Caron 2018; Feliciano and Lanuza 2017; Ichou 2014).

Beyond economic benefits, migration affects outcomes such as well-being, life satisfaction, mental health, stress, self-esteem, etc. These effects are shown to be rather negative. In addition to the costs of geographic movement per se, living in the host country is most often associated with stress and sometimes leads to decreasing levels of well-being. These psychological costs are frequently interpreted as "adaptative" and therefore tightly related to the course of assimilation (Berry et al. 1987; Berry 2001). Some scholars also draw attention to enduring psychological costs for migrants and their offspring that may be related to the experience of hostility and discrimination in the host society (Pascoe and Smart Richman 2009; Safi 2010; Schmitt et al. 2014).

Consequences of migration on physical health have also been extensively studied by research in epidemiology, demography, and sociology (Castañeda et al. 2015). Migrants are often shown to be in better physical shape than natives, which derives from the selective nature of population movements; one needs to be healthy to migrate. The physical health selection of migration is at least partly related to the intrinsic danger of border crossing in contexts where security control has been more and more harmful. If dangerous traversals of natural borders – such as sea crossings in small fishing boats or land crossings hidden in vans, trucks, or ferries – are frequently fatal, attempts to cross artificial ones – such as border walls, barbed-wire fences, and barriers – are just as dangerous. Migration selection is thus partly related to the fact that modern migration kills (Eschbach et al. 1999; Carling 2007).[15]

On the other hand, and despite the fact that those who manage to arrive safely are on average in good shape, this "health premium" is shown to decline over length of stay and across generations due to differential access to the host society's health system and some evidence of direct and indirect discrimination within it. Adopting the "way of life" of the host society sometimes entails less healthy diets and riskier behaviors that may also explain the deterioration of immigrants" physical forms. Some studies also draw attention to the effect of unequal access to health services, structural racism, and discrimination in the medical system (Viruell-Fuentes et al. 2012).

Migration is also shown to affect family structures and relations. In some high emigration societies, one or both parents working abroad is a frequent scenario, with spouses and children left behind. Transnational family life may impact children's development and educational outcomes. Here again, evidence shows variations across family types, countries of origin and socioeconomic backgrounds. The family consequences of migration are also shown to be gendered (Pedraza 1991). Although studies traditionally show married women's migration outcomes to be less positive compared to those of their husbands (in terms of employment, earnings, and occupation; see Boyle et al. 2001) – a result interpreted in relation to the supposedly "tied" nature of women's migration – more recent research insists on the variation in women's benefits from migration depending on marital and educational status (Pessar and Mahler 2003). Some authors also highlight that migration reshapes gender relations within couples, potentially empowering women coming from traditional societies.

In addition to its effects on individuals and families, migration's macro consequences on the host country have been at the center of empirical research, especially in economics. One of the key questions concerns its benefits and costs for the receiving economies. Impacts on growth, employment, and wages have been tackled in a myriad of studies, which sometimes use experimental designs in an attempt to circumvent the difficulty of causal assessment that results from the endogenous nature of migration in relation to economic conditions. These questions are highly politicized, mainly because of fears that immigration may, at least in the short run, have adverse effects on the labor market opportunities of the native population, especially the low-income sector. In the United States, the Mariel boatlift that brought 125,000 Cubans to Miami in 1980 (increasing its labor force by 7 percent) provided a powerful natural experiment. In an influential study, Card (1990) compares the wage trends in Miami to those of similar cities that did not experience migration, concluding that the effects on Miami's labor market were insignificant. American economists have since thoroughly explored this important finding, analyzing its underlying mechanisms or its variations across countries and categories of workers (Borjas 2003; Dustmann et al. 2005, 2009; Aydemir and Borjas 2007). Although there is some variation in the findings across studies, economists nonetheless agree on the fact that the overall labor market effects of migration tend to be slight (Longhi et al. 2005; Hatton 2014). Beyond the US context, Ortega and Peri (2009) confirm this finding using data on 14 OECD destination countries; they also assess positive effects on employment, investments, and GDP.

From another perspective, migration may have considerable impacts on spatial distribution and urban life. Sustained migration reshapes host societies' geographic organization, creating ethnic enclaves and/or "white flight" dynamics and increasing the cosmopolitan nature of cities (Kasinitz et al. 2008; Rathelot and Safi 2013). Migration also affects the national ethnic mix, feeding the perception of the risk of displacement of the majority with potential consequences on social cohesion and civic trust (Alesina and Glaeser 2004). Demographic projections in the United States estimate that the white population will become the minority, quantitatively speaking, by 2040. People of mixed descent also gain demographic and political importance, as shown in the multiracial movement in the United States (Morning 2003; Dacosta 2007). Social scientists have been trying to measure the extent to which these ethnoracial reconfigurations affect preferences for redistribution and the orientation of the welfare state toward egalitarian policies, as well as the provision of public goods (Brady and Finnigan 2013; Alesina, Michalopoulos et al. 2016). On the other hand, diversity in skills and education stemming from migration is shown to promote innovation and economic performance (Alesina, Harnoss et al. 2016; Bove and Elia 2017).

While research traditionally focuses on migration's consequences on the host societies, recent studies increasingly deal with its effect on economic and political conditions in the source countries. This literature is dominated by developmental approaches mainly concerned with impacts on poverty, investments, consumptions, etc. One major empirical issue is related to the measurements of the effects of remittances, which have been dramatically growing during the last decades – estimated at the level of $601 billion, with developing countries receiving $441 billion (World Bank 2016). Although overall effects on economic development and growth seem dependent on whether remittances are used for direct consumption or investments, studies show consistent reduction of poverty levels (Housen et al. 2013). "Social remittances" also garnered attention, especially among sociologists (Levitt 2001); the concept refers to the transfer of cultural patterns and value systems imported from host to sending societies. Transfers may also imply technological innovation, as shown in the case of the Chinese diaspora (Zhou 2009). Finally, the transnational effects of migration on sending societies also touch the political arena: through voting and political organization abroad, emigrants may act as a decisive political lever in some countries.

From another perspective, there is a growing interest in the effect of migration on the levels of economic inequality in sending societies. International migration is costly and selective; access to such an asset is usually restricted to the middle class or the elite, thus reinforcing social inequality in the origin country. Sustained emigration nonetheless lowers the costs for future migrants through network effects, which in turn tend to decrease inequality levels. This U-shaped effect of emigration is measured in several empirical studies (McKenzie and Rapoport 2007).

Research in the same vein is also interested in the effect of migration on the educational level of the home country population. Fears of a "brain drain" mechanism have been quite influential in international institutions and developmental agencies. Here again, robust empirical measurements are rare; recent research nonetheless tends to invalidate a "big" brain drain except in cases of some specific small, high-emigration countries (Docquier and Rapoport 2012). Conversely, emigration seems to enhance investments in education in sending countries, boosting the expected returns for educational credentials. Along with the considerable share of return migrants,[16] some of whom have achieved high levels of education in host countries, these mechanisms may even lead instead to a "brain gain" (Beine et al. 2008).

Finally, global approaches to migration tend to highlight considerable global gains, invalidating the narrow individual and national perspectives. Regardless of national boundaries, worldwide immigration is shown to have considerable global redistributive effects, leading to an increase in overall economic well-being (Clemens 2011; Aubry et al. 2016; Milanovic 2016; Beerli and Peri

2018). It is also strongly tied to innovation, and technological and information transfers. These approaches tend to depict migration as the "great equalizer" of our times; nonetheless, they are hardly audible in the political debate, obviously due to the lack of global political institutionalism. Economic, political, and social interests are very much shaped between and within nation-states, which renders the global gains of migration invisible.

* * *

International migration research has been flourishing over the last decades across a wide range of social science disciplines and approaches. Empirical studies have become more and more sophisticated, and research questions have been constantly refined. My review of this literature inevitably omits several important aspects of the ever-widening scope of migration studies; yet my intention was not to be comprehensive. My aim was to show that this rich literature on patterns, causes, and consequences of migration provides scattered insights on its relation to social inequality. In the rest of the book, I revisit some of these central research questions of the field within an integrated framework that seeks to incorporate migration research within the sociological tradition of social stratification and social inequality scholarship.

– 2 –
Migration and Elementary Mechanisms of Social Inequality: A Conceptual Framework

As shown in Chapter 1, contemporary migration research relates to social inequality in fragmented and multidirectional ways. This chapter aims to outline a unified framework analyzing migration as a case study for inequality theory.

I start by reviewing recent developments in inequality research, focusing on three main questions: "inequality of what?"; "inequality between whom?"; and "how does inequality work?" Relying on the interdisciplinary literature in this field, I emphasize the role of cognitive, cultural, and relational mechanisms in shaping two elementary processes of social stratification: categorization and distribution.

The chapter then discusses the ways in which migration fits within this general conceptualization of social inequality. I distinguish three channels through which migration potentially reshapes inequality: the economic channel stemming from the division of labor, the political channel linked to legal and administrative categorization, and the symbolic channel associated with group boundary-making.

What Is Inequality?

There is undoubtedly a growing concern regarding inequality among academics and policymakers (Neckerman and Torche 2007; Grusky and Ku 2008; Manza and Sauder 2009). Numerous OECD countries experienced stable or decreasing levels of inequality in the post-World War II period, mainly in relation to the expansion of the welfare state. Recent trends conversely suggest a more or less generalized "return of inequality." Piketty's (2014) bestseller is a perfect illustration of this "inequality turn"; it also shows that current concerns overwhelmingly focus on economic inequality (income and wealth). Inequality in the social sciences, however, also encompasses non-economic aspects, as shown in the well-established tradition of "social stratification" studies. Imported from geology, the concept of social stratification refers to the hierarchical structure of societies, a constant feature of human life, although the forms this hierarchy takes have been shown to be various (Sorokin 1927). Social inequality is a narrower concept; it more specifically refers to biased distribution of resources among individuals or social groups.[1] Levels of inequality might thus be considered as a "product" or a "result" of broader stratification dynamics. Social stratification scholarship aims at both describing the "state" of the distribution of resources (i.e., the levels of inequality) and also identifying the mechanisms involved in its production and reproduction (the making of inequality).

For the sake of summarizing recent developments in social stratification theory, it is possible to delineate three key questions:

1   The first is related to the type of resources that concern the theory of social stratification (inequality of what?).
2   The second focuses on "who" gets "what." It identifies groups that are relevant to the analysis of the unequal distribution of these resources (inequality between whom?).
3   The mechanisms relating to the production and reproduction of inequality are addressed by the third question (how does inequality work?).

These three basic questions were strongly intertwined in classical approaches to social stratification. Given the rapid industrialization of Western societies and the profound changes in the division of labor, which shaped the context of the earliest stratification approaches in the social sciences, the focus has traditionally been on the distribution of economic resources. The Marxian scheme probably provides the most integrated synthesis of these three key questions. Marx's analysis of social inequality in industrialized societies is anchored in the sphere of production where material resources are produced (*inequality of what?*). Income-generating labor market activities and the division of labor they entail (i.e., the relations of production, to use Marx's term) form the process that defines group categorization and social positions or classes (*inequality between whom?*), as well as the mechanism through which the unequal distribution of resources operates between these groups (*how does inequality work?*). In other words, the division of labor per se is the locus of resource production, the process that categorizes groups and the mechanism by which these resources are unevenly distributed among these groups. Group categorization into social classes is thus endogenous to the process of resource distribution; in Tilly's (1998) words, capitalists and workers are "internal categories."

Conversely, recent developments tend to highlight the analytic usefulness of the separation between the three questions. This helps to explain not only the existence of inequalities, but also their durability (Tilly 1998). A theory of social stratification must account for the ways in which inequalities resist and recur, and explain why agents tend to accept them. The separation between the questions of *what*, *whom*, and *how* also emanates from attempts to reconcile the micro and macro foundations of social stratification theory and to confer upon social agents a crucial role in the production and reproduction of inequality (Small et al. 2010; Lamont et al. 2014). The following sections delve further into the conceptualization of the three key inequality questions.

Inequality of what?

Recent developments in inequality theory can first be understood as directly linked to the increasing complexity of the answer to the first question, the "what" question, through the expansion of social inequality analysis to non-material rewards. While the material/non-material dichotomy has some limitations, as shown by studies on inequalities in health, lifespan, or sexuality, it has the merit of emphasizing dimensions of inequality that are unrelated to income. The spectrum of resources viewed as relevant to inequality studies nonetheless differs among social scientists. The discipline of economics was founded around reflections on the distribution of income and wealth and the role of the market in the writing of early figures such as Adam Smith and David Ricardo. Studies in evolutionary anthropology distinguish between "embodied" and "extrasomatic" capitals as main inequality factors and insist on "human capital" as being the increasingly influential current form of the embodied capital (Bowles et al. 2010; Kaplan et al. 2011). In sociology, classical distinctions between Marx's and Weber's views on inequality highlight power and status as central components of social stratification in addition to class. In a seminal contribution, Bourdieu (1986) builds on a multidimensional conception of capital, disentangling three non-economic types of capital: social (returns related to relationships and networks), cultural (returns related to education not only as certificates but also as "habitus" and relations to "cultural articles"), and symbolic (returns of classifications and categories of perception in terms of power). While Bourdieu's original contribution emphasizes the cumulative nature of these conceptions of capital, some may find it overly generalized in its post-Bourdieusian use (cognitive capital, spatial capital, erotic capital, ethnic capital, autochthonous capital, etc.). In their summary of social stratification forms in human societies, Grusky and Ku (2008) distinguish eight broad types of resources: economic, political, cultural, social, honorary, civil, human, and physical. All in all, the increasingly shared acceptance of the multidimensionality of resources opens the analysis in terms of inequality to virtually all social phenomena (including power, respect, dignity, prestige, recognition, love, affection, friendship, lifestyles, phenotypes, cultures, etc.). Sen's (1979) widely used principle of equality of "capabilities to function fully as a human being" aims at capturing this multidimensionality. The concept of stratification refers to the full range of inequality sources operating in an interconnected system.

Nonetheless, differences in attributes cannot always be interpreted in terms of resources that are relevant to the study of inequality. Adopting a historical approach, Tilly (2003) defines inequality as the result of unequal control over value-producing resources; this means that attributes that contribute to a flow of valued goods or services are those that are central to inequality studies. Value-producing resources have varied throughout human history: Tilly analyzes historical examples such as spices, animals, lands, human labor, commitment-maintaining institutions, machines, etc. He highlights financial capital, information, sciences, and media as the main value-producing resources involved in contemporary inequality dynamics. Types of stratification regimes derive directly from the nature of the resources that are principally at stake: self-ownership in slavery societies, lands in feudal systems, labor and capital in industrialized societies, human capital and knowledge in post-industrialized ones, etc. Beyond the economic concept of rarity, this multidimensional approach pays attention to the collective, cultural, and institutional mechanisms that define certain resources as valuable and desirable. Research on the "moral economy" (economy based on local and contextual representations of social justice), on the one hand, and on "inefficient markets," on the other, suggest that these mechanisms are at least as decisive as general equilibrium market mechanisms (Akerlof 1970, 2000; Thompson 1971; Scott 1976).

Inequality between whom?

Individual analysis of inequality in terms of a continuous distribution of assets and attributes is powerful in providing straightforward and comparable measures; take, for instance, the recent attempts to measure income inequality worldwide using individual data (Milanovic 2005, 2016). Yet it comes at the cost of a great deal of abstraction. When we interact with people in everyday life, we hardly locate them on the full spectrum of income distribution. Instead, we tend to associate others with a discrete and limited number of categories, even when these classifications pertain to income. Moreover, in addition to perceiving that we are dealing with rich or middle-income persons, broadly speaking, we also tend to classify our protagonists in social interactions according to other types of categories (gender, race, age, sexual orientation, psychological traits, physical traits, etc.) depending on their relevance within social settings. The processes that group humans, whether they are coercive, technological, legal, cultural, or cognitive, are thus operative factors of inequality. In parallel to the acknowledgment of the diversity of resources, the idea that groups that are relevant to the analysis of social stratification in complex modern societies are themselves varied is widely accepted.

As highlighted by Tilly (2003), categorical inequality challenges the simple and widespread model of inequality conceived in terms of "competitive sorting," which posits that individual differences in attributes are evaluated and ordered through organized social processes such as tryouts, auditions, and elections. This model tends to justify inequality as efficient and fair. Only a few social spheres nonetheless comply with such a model: elitist universities, some artistic fields such as music and dance, sports such as football, etc. Most inequality-generating processes instead rely on categorical distinctions that facilitate the matching of individuals to social positions, thus increasing the durability of inequality and solidifying social stratification systems. Categorical inequality makes control over access to resources more efficient, facilitating unequal treatments from both inside and outside members. In most situations involving access to resources, matching individuals to social positions hardly relies on individual-to-individual scrutiny but rather stems from assignment to and recruitment within readily available social categories that function as labels, markers, or cognitive shortcuts (educational level, gender, race, age, phenotype, citizenship, ethnicity, etc.).

Inequality is thus embedded in categorical distinctions that may exist outside and prior to market relations and function as channels through which resources, opportunities and benefits are drained into the possession of dominant groups (Tilly 1998; Massey 2007). These categories are often imported into organizations and built into laws, regulations, institutions, and markets; they "map" social relations.

The categorical turn not only means that inequality scholarship should pay specific attention to the distribution of resources between social categories, but also, and perhaps most importantly, it suggests that the study of social inequality cannot do without the analysis of social categorization per se. Categorization is indeed constitutive of social stratification mechanisms. It refers to a set of processes that proceed by classification and allocation to categories, sorting individuals, spaces, positions, actions, ideas, and so on (Bowker and Star 2000). Although social differences often function as grounds for categorization, they do not always produce categorical inequality. The relationship between differences and inequality is contingent upon and subject to variations over time and contexts. Lamont and Molnar (2002: 168) write about the transformation of "symbolic boundaries" ("conceptual distinctions made by social actors to categorize objects, people, and practices") into "social boundaries" ("objectified forms of social differences manifested in unequal access to and unequal distribution of resources and social opportunities"). As shown in this definition, it is as though social inequality is linked to certain categorical distinctions that become meaningful and powerful in specific social settings.

As a consequence of this categorical turn, inequality studies have been increasingly concerned with analyzing the relevance of certain specific social categories in shaping inequality dynamics across a variety of social contexts (Brubaker 2015). A classic distinction is the one that differentiates between characteristics that are perceived as *ascriptive* (such as sex, age, phenotypes, disability, place of birth, etc.) and those that are *achieved* (education, occupation, residential location, etc.).[2] The intersectional approach consists of bridging the gaps between specific group-level dimensions of inequality in order to uncover their common (or sometimes distinct) mechanisms and highlight the ways in which they interrelate in creating complex inequality (Crenshaw 1991; McCall 2001; Ridgeway and Kricheli-Katz 2013). While social class has traditionally been at the center of the literature on social stratification, it became very common to combine approaches in terms of class, race, gender, skin color, citizenship, sexual orientation, etc. The class/race/gender trio has been shown to be pivotal in the United States and, with varying composition, in most contemporary societies (Boris and Janssens 1999; Charles 2008; Grusky et al. 2008).

Interdisciplinary research on inequality has developed rapidly over these last decades, analyzing the underlying mechanisms of social categorization. These are shown to be multileveled: cognitive mechanisms (at the micro level), cultural and organizational mechanisms (at the meso level) and institutional and structural mechanisms (at the macro level) overlap in producing and sustaining social categories. Social psychological research highlights the cognitive individual bases of categorization, emphasizing its intrinsic relationship to the ways in which the human brain processes information. Social cognition research has documented the role of stereotypes, beliefs, and expectations related to social differences in the way people make sense of, coordinate with and relate to others (Fiske and Taylor 1991; Fiske 1998; Ridgeway and Correll 2006; Ridgeway 2014). Simplified cultural codes are the most cognitively effective, since they apply to virtually everybody in the course of defining "self" and "other" in social interactions; social psychologists call them the "primary frame for social relations" (Ridgeway 2011). Empirical research suggests that sex, race, and age are primary categories of person perception in several contemporary societies. This means that most other person-related categorizations are nested within prior classifications as male/female, black/white/Asian/Latino, young/old. To the extent that they are salient in social settings, these primary frames therefore bias expectations in terms of status, evaluation of performance and attributions of ability (Berger and Webster 2006).

Sociologists often insist on the collective and cultural dimensions of categorization (Lamont 1999; Small et al. 2010). Bullock (2008) describes how the dynamics between race, ethnicity, gender, and class in the United States are shaped by core ideologies such as individualism, meritocracy, equality of opportunity, and upward mobility. Lamont thoroughly discusses cultural mechanisms of categorical inequality in her book *The Dignity of Working Men* (2000), in which she shows that different narratives produce different symbolic boundaries between social groups in France and the United States, thus creating various grounds for social inequality (see also Lamont and Duvoux 2014). This cultural approach to categorization is also eminently historical. This means that categories of inequality are not in themselves immanent or natural; they stem from social construction processes that confer upon them a shared meaning. In other words, the categories relevant to the analysis of social stratification are part of what is "taken for granted" in social interactions and constitute "common knowledge" (Chwe 2001). They relate to frames, narratives, or repertoires that govern meaning-making processes in social life.

Categorization processes are highly dependent on social contexts. On the macro level, profound ideological, technological, or institutional transformations may lead to categorization "shocks" or gradual transformation. Tilly (2005) provides historical examples such as encounters (newcomers and old settlers), imposition (police and administrative categories), negotiation (gangs, gender, race), and transfer across social settings (across cities, countries, from the family to the workplace, etc.). Since categorization processes occur and reproduce within social interactions, the meso context is at least equally important. By providing stable frames, rules, and routines for social interactions, institutions and organizations in general warrant the sustainability of inequality (households, neighborhoods, firms, schools, universities, states, etc.) (Tomaskovic-Devey 1993, 2014; Tomaskovic-Devey et al. 2006; McTague et al. 2009). Goal-oriented relational contexts, of which the most powerful example in modern societies is the workplace, play a crucial role in generating and sustaining categorical inequality.

How does inequality work?

Once the "between whom" question is dealt with, the "how" question relates to uncovering the processes that allocate resources between social categories that are relevant to inequality studies.

Although the vocabulary of inequality is quite broad (domination, oppression, discrimination, segregation, etc.), there is a certain consensus that exploitation and exclusion (or opportunity hoarding) are the most central mechanisms (Tilly 1998; Massey 2007). They allow us to interpret various historical phases of social stratification. Exploitation is based on the extraction of benefits from the work or effort of others. It is a central mechanism in the classical Marxian frame. Opportunity hoarding refers to the exclusion of others from areas of resources and opportunities. It was highlighted in the work of Weber, who referred to social closure and monopoly as crucial mechanisms of inequality. Exploitation and opportunity hoarding are ideal-typical mechanisms; they often combine in channeling previously sorted people to a set of social positions or unequal opportunity spheres. Even within the most orthodox approaches to exploitation (i.e., the Marxian scheme), exclusion is far from being out of the picture. Private property rights are indispensable to exploitation: they function as a prerequisite exclusionary mechanism preventing the "exploited" (the workers) from access to resources (capital) (Wright 1997: 10). The increasing analysis of inequality in terms of rent also involves both exclusion and exploitation components. Sorenson (2000) highlights examples such as industrial monopolies, retention of information, rents linked to expertise or qualifications, cultural rents, and so on, which provide the exclusionary basis for further exploitation.

Nonetheless, distinguishing between the two mechanisms remains heuristic, because the degree to which one or the other is predominant may affect social relations within unequal settings. Wright (1997) differentiates between exploitative and non-exploitative oppression; the former implies interdependence between the exploiter and the exploited, whereas the latter is potentially conducive to the elimination of the oppressed by the oppressor.[3] This might explain why racial relations more often entail physical forms of exclusion and domination. Social sciences studies show, for example, that spatial segregation (Massey and Denton 1993; Sharkey 2013) and, more recently, mass incarceration (Western 2006; Western and Pettit 2010) have been pivotal to racial inequality in the United States; both practices are mostly exclusive. This may also explain why mass experiences of group eliminations and genocides are most frequently related to ethnoracial relations (the extermination of indigenous populations in the Americas, the Nazi genocide and, more recently, the genocide in Rwanda are powerful examples) (Wacquant 1997; Brubaker and Laitin 1998; Wimmer 2013).

Although the centrality of exploitation and exclusion is widely accepted in inequality theory, some scholars reflect on additional mechanisms. Therborn (2013), for instance, stresses distantiation as a central mechanism; it is a process of a group moving apart from the rest, "discerning winners from losers." Deaton (2015) refers to a similar type of mechanism in the "story" he tells of the "great escape." In his view, distantiation is a central type of inequality driven by innovation and biased technological progress. Distantiation as the "great escape story" may be regarded as a form of exclusion of others from areas of opportunity and progress, although this exclusive process may not be intentional. Exclusion from access to medical knowledge is a powerful example; health is one of the major "killing fields of inequality" (Wilkinson 2005; Therborn 2013), and health inequality mainly derives from unequal exposure to risk and unequal access to care. Other mechanisms have been described in the literature: evaluation and hierarchization, claim-making, and resource pooling, etc. (Lamont 2012; Lamont et al. 2014; Tomaskovic-Devey 2014). All in all, if they introduce interesting nuances, all these mechanisms lend themselves to a basic analysis in terms of a combination of exploitation and exclusion. The latter are indeed two fundamental mechanisms through which resource allocation can be distorted: exclude others from access to existing resources, or use the work and effort of others to scoop up and monopolize new resources.

While exploitation and exclusion have traditionally been analyzed in a macro-theoretical fashion, contemporary scholarship is characterized by a more pronounced inclination to think of them as being embedded in social relations (Tilly 2001a; Tomaskovic-Devey 2014). Tilly speaks of "relational realism," considering that "transactions, interactions, social ties, and conversations constitute the central stuff of social life" (2002: 72). This relational conception of inequality emphasizes the "doing-together" processes that generate it. It draws attention to the need for any theory of social stratification to identify spaces of stable interactions where resource distribution biases are routinely at play producing and reproducing sustainable inequalities. It is within these relational contexts, which function as *inequality regimes* (Acker 2006), that individuals encounter and engage in social relations in which resources (money, power, respect, etc.) are more or less unevenly distributed. This means that inequality cannot be fully understood by focusing only on one group (the dominant, the top income, males, whites). Rather, the focus should be on the interaction between groups (Blumer 1958; Blau 1977; Collins 2005). A consequence of this methodological interactionism is the identification of institutionalized spaces of encounters that become "durable social networks" (Tomaskovic-Devey 2014: 68). These spaces reproduce certain forms of interactions and thus make the unequal processes of distribution within them sustainable. Contexts such as firms, households, neighborhoods, schools, etc. consequently form convenient platforms for empirical research on inequality.

Toward an Elementary Framework for the Study of Inequality

The separation between the *what*, *whom*, and *how* questions allows us to sketch a general framework for the study of inequality. This framework is based on the mutual relations between two central processes that feed inequality dynamics: categorization and distribution (see Figure 2.1). It should nonetheless be emphasized that the distinction between these two processes is mainly heuristic; in practice, it is quite hard to separate that which categorizes from that which distributes. The processes of resource distribution are themselves categorization processes; they create resource-endowed and resource-deprived categories. As mentioned above, social class, one of the main categorizations studied in sociology, is endogenous to the distribution of resources. And as discussed below, legal classification provides another example of such imbrication between categorization and distribution.

Moreover, the separation between categorization and distribution is mostly analytical, because even in situations where inequality originally more heavily derives from one or the other, the two processes often end up mutually affecting each other (represented by the double-oriented arrows in Figure 2.1). By mobilizing experimental protocols, social psychologists show that when a categorization system is shared by the actors, even if it is fundamentally disconnected from the sphere of resources, it is likely to lead to biased behavior, thus ultimately affecting resource distribution. Tajfel's seminal contribution to the theory of social identity clearly shows that the behavior of agents in favor of their group (*group-favoritism*) can create de facto inequalities, even when these groups are constructed in a quite arbitrary way and are disconnected from the distribution of resources (the red and the blue teams defined in a game organized within an experimental design, for instance) (Tajfel 1981; Tajfel and Turner 1986).[4]

Research in this vein also shows that the salience of social categories and their cognitive power affect the degree to which the distribution of resources becomes biased among them. The market, which is the locus of production and distribution of material resources, often consolidates categorical inequality originating outside the market (i.e., exogenous categorizations produced by historical processes such as colonization, wars, etc.). More fundamentally – and this is a key point in the contribution of the categorical approach to the theory of social stratification, instilled by cultural mechanisms of disputes, negotiations, and struggles for classification – the evolution of categorization processes can ultimately affect the distribution of resources among social categories: for example, the US Civil Rights Movement can be understood as the result of a long process of challenging or renegotiating racial categorization (Omi and Winant 1994), which ultimately modified the distribution of not only legal, moral, and symbolic resources, but also economic, spatial, and, more generally, material resources between white and black Americans. Feminist movements and their consequences to the evolution of gender equality in the labor market may be interpreted in the same vein.

Conversely, a high degree of inequality in the distribution of resources is likely to solidify exogenous categories. As discussed by Ridgeway (2014), when correlated with levels of resource endowments, social categories such as gender and race generate differences in status: they acquire symbolic and moral meanings (honor, esteem, respect) that come into play in the reproduction of inequality. This means that people make status beliefs about social categories that possess more or fewer resources: the haves are perceived as "better" and "more competent" than the have-nots, which provides a powerful form of legitimizing social inequality. Ridgeway describes how these "status biases" become autonomous mechanisms independent from the control of resources, not only stabilizing but also feeding social inequality. In brief, it is precisely within this close articulation between processes of categorization and distribution that the durability of inequality lies.

This brings me to a final point before moving on to analyzing the relation between migration and inequality. It must be noted that this global framework of inequality ought to be understood as processual. Social structure or social inequalities are sometimes produced by continuous, recursive, and cumulative interactions between categorization and distribution. Thus, inequality can hardly be conceived as an equilibrium; rather, it is a continual self-feeding and cumulative process. This processual perspective has implications for the very design of empirical research, which should seek to decompose and disentangle underlying mechanisms in the generation and reproduction of inequality (Tilly 2001b; Reskin 2003). The focus on mechanisms must not, however, be to the detriment of the description of the social structure as a whole. The idea of circularity refers to this link between the structure of stratification (patterns and levels of inequality) and its generating and reproducing mechanisms. As Abbott (2003, 2001) points out, circularity specifically refers to the interdependence between social stratification as a structure and the mechanisms involved in its production. The contribution of sociology might appear to be potentially decisive in this regard, in comparison with more specialized disciplines (that focus solely on micro or macro levels).

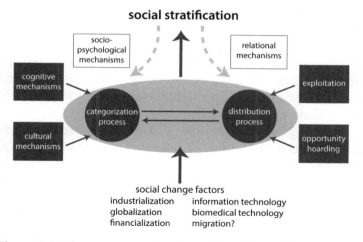

Figure 2.1 Elementary mechanisms of social stratification

Figure 2.1 attempts to synthesize the dynamics of social stratification described in the contemporary research reviewed above. The structure of social stratification at a time *t* is the result of the long-term combination of two processes: categorization and distribution. These two processes affect each other: distribution endogenously creates categories, and categorization that might be initially disconnected from the distribution of resources is likely to affect the latter. These two processes must therefore be understood as a system. This system holds thanks to cognitive and cultural mechanisms that drive categorization, and exploitative and exclusionary mechanisms that bias the distribution of resources. The processes of categorization and distribution are eminently relational, and it is their embeddedness in organized contexts of social interactions (neighborhoods, firms, households, etc.) that guarantees their sustainability. Social stratification at time *t* has a decisive effect on the relational context;[5] it constitutes a structure of opportunity, in turn affecting the processes of categorization and distribution (broken line arrows). In other terms, levels of inequality predetermine the context of interactions (more or less salient separation between groups in workplaces, neighborhoods, social relations, etc.), thus affecting the evolution of inequality. Hence, the figure clearly shows that levels of inequality are both the consequences of elementary mechanisms and the precondition of the durability of any unequal system. Finally, it provides some examples of the factors of change traditionally analyzed in the literature as affecting stratification dynamics.

Disentangling mechanisms of inequality inevitably leads to highlighting mechanisms of equalization. The distinction between categorization and distribution in particular has some policy implications. Combating inequalities can be achieved through two general channels: working on categorizations or altering the distribution of resources. De-categorization is usually driven by cultural negotiations that gradually change the social meaning of social categories (e.g., the role of cultural shifts in the attenuation of gender inequality), whereas reducing the unequal allocation of resources requires targeting the very mechanisms of distribution or correcting for their outcomes (via equalizing positions or redistributing). It goes without saying that these two dimensions of egalitarian instruments interact closely; some types of affirmative policies, for example, affect categorization (through recognition and rehabilitation) while redistributing resources and opportunities. The mutually feeding effects of the correlation between symbolic positions within the categorization process and social positions within the distribution of resources – or, in other words, the fact that differences in income, wealth, and education are sizeable between social categories based on gender, race and ethnicity – advocate in favor of large-scale actions that seek to equalize social positions insofar as, by reducing this correlation itself, these policies bring about dynamics of de-categorization in the long term.[6] From this point of view, the "equalizing outcome approach" may seem to be one of the most efficient in order to "equalize opportunity" (McCall 2016). Nonetheless, one may alternatively argue that de-categorization leads to the attenuation of biases in distribution in a deeper and more lasting way, delegitimizing the very source of biased distribution. Inclusive policies that directly target group boundaries may in this respect appear to be the most valuable to creating egalitarian dynamics (Therborn 2013). In short, uncovering the mechanisms that contribute to creating inequalities also highlights the ways in which political struggles and efficient policies may potentially undo inequality.

Migration: A Case Study for Inequality Research

In exploring the analytical channels that link migration to social inequality, it is useful to separate the effect of migration on the processes of resource distribution from its impact on categorization. This approach bridges the gap between migration studies, ethnic and racial studies, and social stratification studies.

First, and most importantly, migration is a particularly interesting case for the study of inequality because it potentially affects each of the aforementioned elementary processes, thus providing examples of endogenous categorization/distribution. Migration is indeed directly linked to the process of division of labor as long as we extend our conceptualization of this process beyond the nation-state. Labor-oriented approaches to migration focus on the global labor–migration nexus, shedding light on the role of structural factors such as profit-accumulative capitalism and market globalization in driving human migration. The global division of labor thus produces a worldwide categorization of workers upon which the migrant labor industry is based. Similar to what has been discussed above, this migration-driven categorization of workers may be regarded as an "endogenous categorization." Chapter 3 is dedicated to precisely this channel – the economic channel – through which migration reshapes inequality.

Interestingly, migration provides an additional powerful example of endogenous categorization.

Migration is directly related to legal and administrative types of categorizations, which define categories while at the same time unevenly distributing resources (such as rights and political status). Modern migration indeed involves distribution/categorization dynamics that allocate humans to administrative categories, which leads directly to the unequal distribution of resources between these categories. Distinguishing between nationals and foreigners, citizenship might be the most powerful example of this, although other related migration categorizations are increasingly important (permanent residents, economic migrants, family reunion migrants, refugees and asylum seekers, undocumented migrants, etc.). These formal categorizations are legally dictated and administratively defined; they create sharp boundaries between insiders and outsiders, rigidifying inequality. I will examine the dynamics of this legal channel through which migration relates to inequality in greater detail in Chapter 4.

Finally, I will argue in Chapter 5 that migration's effects on inequality also go through categorization processes that remain relatively independent of resource distribution. This is indeed the case, because migration directly intervenes in the formation and transformation of ethnoracial boundaries. These boundaries may be seen as the ensuing symbolic struggle and negotiation over human classifications on the local and global level, thus contributing to inequality dynamics in multileveled perspectives.

Table 2.1 summarizes the three main channels that link migration to inequality dynamics. For each channel, I highlight the categorization and distribution processes at stake, while trying to provide answers to the three inequality questions raised above (what, whom, how). I also provide some examples that will be fully discussed in each of the corresponding chapters. The three channels involve three types of categorizations of migrants: as types of workers, types of citizens, and types of humans. In the economic channel, exploitation is the most central mechanism through which migration reshapes inequality. In the legal and ethnoracial channels, opportunity hoarding seems to be more pivotal. These three channels have the particularity to be operational at the national and transnational levels. One can discern here that migration is an essential contribution to inequality scholarship; it forces us to broaden the analysis beyond the country level, while both migration and inequality studies have long been subject to "national methodologism" (Wimmer and Schiller 2003). The three processes of inequalities related to migration are indeed fundamentally transnational. Neither the division of labor nor legal categorization can be understood within the paradigm of the "container-state': the former channel takes on a global political economy approach, and the second obliges us to rethink the concept of citizenship as embedded in the categorization of cross-border movements and transnational processes. As for the ethnoracial channel, it lends itself to a diversity of localizations: the effect of migration on the dynamics of ethnoracial formation may be operational on the national (minority groups), subnational (ethnic enclaves, ethnic neighborhoods), and transnational levels (diaspora, return

Table 2.1 The three channels through which migration affects inequality dynamics

	Inequality of what?	Inequality between whom?	How does inequality work?	Examples
Economic channel	Labor and socioeconomic positions	Categories of workers, migrant/ native labor, international social classes	Endogenous distribution of economic resources, global division of labor, exploitation	Post-World War II European guest workers migration Contemporary care workers migration
Legal channel	Rights, legal and political status	Legally enforced categories of citizens	Endogenous legal and administrative categorizations (border control, citizenship law, alien law, etc.), opportunity hoarding	Undocumented migrants Refugees, family reunion, economic migrants Biomedical categorization of migrants
Ethnoracial channel	Status, moral worth, respect	Ethnic/racial/ national categories of humans	Group boundary-making and ethnoracial formation. Potentially expanding to legal and socioeconomic inequalities, opportunity hoarding	The reconfiguration of white/black/ Hispanic racial boundaries in the US Transnational transfer of ethnoracial categorizations

and circular migrants). Reflecting on the ways in which migration affects inequality dynamics thus urges us to think of inequalities as produced by categorization/distribution systems that operate at multilevel scales. Looking at the world as a whole rather than as a constellation of nation-states deeply changes the perspective of inequality. More specifically, restricting equality of opportunity, a dominant philosophical principle of justice in modern democracies, to the nation-state level is no more defensible when the concept of justice acquires a global scope. One of the most important benefits of studying international migration through a lens of inequality lies precisely in challenging the nationally established paradigms of social justice.

− 3 −

The Economic Channel: Migrant Workers in the Global Division of Labor

This chapter focuses on the economic channel through which migration affects inequality dynamics. It first reviews a diverse body of research in sociology, political economy, labor economics, and international trade that contributes to our understanding of this channel. Despite sharp variations in theoretical assumptions, these fields of study clearly anchor migration in large-scale economic dynamics and the study of the labor market. One can generally distinguish between global and national/local approaches within this broad literature. The global approach draws a direct line between migration and the structural tensions and transformations that are characteristic of capitalist economies. Importing migrant labor is understood, in a rather functionalist fashion, as a "solution" to the structural failures of capitalism. Some scholars further conceptualize the importation of labor through migration as an "exploitative technology," or draw lines between migrant labor and domination processes anchored in world-system relations. The local and national approaches are mostly concerned with the effects of migration on labor market equilibriums (unemployment and wages) with an attempt to take into account the selectivity of migrant workers in terms of human capital and its consequences for different segments of the labor force (native high-skilled versus low-skilled workers, female workers, earlier migrants, minority workers, etc.). Regardless of their theoretical affiliations, these approaches share an understanding of migration as related to the global division of labor with direct implications in terms of the distribution of economic, labor-based resources. This process of unequal distribution also simultaneously creates migrant categories of workers that can be understood as "transnational social classes.'

Finally, the chapter discusses the ways in which these approaches lead to a cross-fertilization between migration research and the study of labor market inequality. Framing migration as exclusively linked to economic determinants nonetheless suffers from some limitations, which I will address in the last section.

Migrants in the Global Division of Labor

The economic channel has its roots in the interference between migration and the division of labor, the latter being regarded as the central distributional process that allocates jobs, economic rewards and socioeconomic positions. Social science research that investigates this economic channel is concentrated into three disciplinary fields that rarely interact: labor and industrial economics, political economy, and sociology. This literature varies in the scope of analysis (the global economy, national labor markets, cities, firms, etc.) and in the specific labor market inequality being scrutinized (the migrant/native gap, inequality among native workers, inequality among migrant workers, gender and ethnoracial inequality). Nonetheless, and despite this heterogeneity of perspectives, this body of research intrinsically deals with migration as a source of labor; migration reshapes the division of labor and affects the allocation of different "types of jobs" and the uneven rewards that are associated with them, which endogenously categorizes migrants as "types of workers."

Migration and labor market adjustments

Migration studies have a close connection to the analysis of capitalism in the social sciences. To understand these theoretical perspectives, it is useful to start with Marx and his approach to economic inequality in industrial societies. According to Marx, the transition from feudalism to capitalism took shape in the detachment of the peasants from their means of production (their soil) and the "upheaval" of the working class formed of "great masses of men ... hurled into the labor market as free, unprotected and rightless proletarians" (1976: 876). Former peasants had to leave their villages and "move" in order to be "hurled into the labor market," thus providing the labor force that was necessary for the expansion of capitalism. The geographic mobility of workers is closely related to this commodification of labor. Urbanization constitutes a reference case in this regard, illustrating the extent to which human mobility (including international migration) is embedded in the emergence, development, and ongoing evolutions of capitalism. Peasants' "rural exodus" is a stylized fact that came along with industrialization, despite some variations in scope and timing over the two last centuries. Regardless of the distance and the borders that are crossed, worker mobility is related to the necessary encounters of this structural supply of "free labor" that has to "follow" the labor market, on the one hand, and the structural demand of low-cost production and service provision that is characteristic of capitalism, on the other. While rural exodus has occurred in the midst of the transition from feudalism to capitalism in many Western societies, later developments of capitalism continued to rely on workers' geographic mobility in the search for profit. In the first half of the twentieth century, "modern" slavery, which can be regarded as a forced-migration industry, was studied within this general macro perspective that analyzed the economic dynamics of capitalism – for example, in the works of Williams (1944) and Cox (1948). Slavery certainly represents an extreme case study, but it is highly emblematic of the intrinsic relations between "migrant labor" and stratification regimes. Migration, in the case of slavery, produced the "types of workers" (slaves) characteristic of slave-based economies. In more orthodox Marxist terms, worker migration is a "technique" that provides the "industrial reserve army" that capitalism needs to enhance the efficiency of the extraction of "capitalist surplus" from the "exploited" labor force (other techniques include lengthening the working day, capital destruction, internationalization of the production process, etc.) (Castles and Kosack 1973; DeFreitas 1991). The term "technique" here encompasses a whole range of tools and devices involved in worker mobility management, whether relying on physical coercion and/or on techno-logical innovations (as for shipping in slavery periods, for instance). Contemporary techniques mainly rely on law and regulation types of "devices" that establish different forms of "labor controls" on migrant workers, while the overt use of violence, although not negligible, has become rarer.[1] International migration thus feeds a "labor repressive system" that, though varied in its patterns, is characteristic of capitalist economies (Miles 1984, 1989; Anderson 2000, 2010; Cohen 2006; Brown et al. 2009). These theoretical insights may appear to fit the "great age of migration" that channeled workers to the "new world" at the turn of the twentieth century. They also find sharp resonance in the massive and organized nature of the use of migrant labor in many European countries after World War II (France, Germany, and the United Kingdom in particular) (Noiriel 1984; Hollifield 1992; Green 2002; McDowell 2009; Long 2014). These migrants were clearly conceived as flexible, temporary workers (guest workers) and were often hired by state agencies directly in the source country in order to fill the demand for labor, particularly in the industrial and construction sectors. This form of tied labor, which sometimes explicitly links workers' entry to the employer's identity (i.e., employer sponsorship), still exists in many immigration societies, with considerable power in the hands of employers and clear evidence of migrant worker exploitation (Castles and Kosack 1973; Longva 1999).

While these Marxian perspectives could be interpreted as assigning a "functionalist" role to migration, in the sense that it serves to enhance capitalism's profitability, it is within the industrial relations research field that the relation between migrant labor and the organization and regulation of the labor market started to be systematically investigated. The theory of duality of labor markets brings the "political struggle" over "who will bear the cost" of structural uncertainty in capitalist economies into the picture (Doeringer and Piore 1971). Yet this approach has a functionalist flavor as well, since it is the intrinsic tensions of capitalism that lead to the segmentation of the labor market into two sectors: a primary sector, containing better paying, more stable and otherwise attractive job opportunities, and the more privileged members of the labor force; and a secondary sector, containing generally poor paying, insecure, and unattractive jobs. Migrants (along with women, youth, and other disadvantaged groups) form the bulk of the secondary sector. As stated quite clearly by Piore, the dualism of the labor market is originally anchored in the basic antagonism between capital and labor, the latter being used to top up most of capitalism's structural maladjustments. Nonetheless, this intrinsic capital/labor dualism takes different forms depending on industries, sectors, and social and political contexts. This heterogeneity results in a diversity of "institutional arrangements" that are aimed at securing the "primary sector" and/or flexibilizing the "secondary sector" (see, for example, Piore's [1978] comparison between the French and Italian institutional arrangements in the 1960s). Immigration regulations within national economies could be understood as the results of these institutional arrangements.

While these economics-driven approaches to migration are tailored to a pattern of massive postwar labor migration to Europe, they also seem useful in the study of contemporary migration in the service and care sectors. Some professions that are predominantly made up of migrant labor are portrayed as *migratory industries* (the care sector, household services, the construction sector, and some other industrial sectors in particular). Nonetheless, certain high-skilled economic sectors also rely on forms of migratory industries; information and computer technologies are among the most studied, but medicine, engineering, and other high-skilled occupations increasingly employ migrants. The overrepresentation of migrants at the top of the skills distribution has indeed become a stylized fact in many immigration countries; recent accounts show that, in 17 of 29 selected OECD countries, the proportion of highly educated workers is greater among the foreign born than among the native born (OECD 2018: 94). This pattern is particularly salient in Canada, Australia, and the United Kingdom. In the United States, the proportion of foreigners in STEM occupations (sciences, technology, engineering, math) has steadily increased since the 1990s, exceeding 60 percent among those with a PhD (Hanson and Slaughter 2016). The success of Amazon, Facebook, Google, Microsoft, etc. is thus to be linked to the ability of the US economy to import this high-skilled labor from abroad.

Moreover, and in addition to the direct involvement of corporations, the state-organized feature of migration is most manifest today in those immigration policies that aim at attracting high-skilled workers (points-based systems in the United Kingdom, Australia, Canada; the EU Blue Card, etc.). It is notable, for instance, that the design of the intra-Europe free movement policy and its coupling with the harmonization of a university education is tailored to enhance the mobility of the highly skilled (Cerna 2008; Triandafyllidou and Isaakyan 2014; Kalantaryan and Martin 2015). Although high-skilled migration helps put into perspective the representation of migrant labor as being disadvantaged and vulnerable, its relation to the economic channel of inequality is similar on most lines to low-skilled labor migration. High-skilled migrant labor is also used to alleviate intrinsic tensions of capitalist regimes that are nonetheless analyzed as related to skill-biased technological change (SBTC), a different version of structural maladjustments in labor/capital interdependency. SBTC is considerable within the information and communication sector, thus contributing to the widening skill premium within it (measured in the United States for the college-educated since the 1980s) (Violante et al. 2016). While high-skilled migrants imported to fill these gaps tend to be portrayed as "the cosmopolitan elite," evidence of downgrading and lower wages in comparison with native high-skilled workers points to their relative exploitation. Even the relatively advantaged STEM workers in the United States experience wage gaps, though to a lesser extent and with less durability than for the average foreign-born worker. Hanson and Slaughter (2016) show that it takes 10 years of labor market experience in the United States for immigrants in STEM occupations to earn equal to or more than native-born workers doing similar tasks. Finally, one may further argue that the migrant labor approach also applies to student migration, which represents a growing share of migration in industrialized countries, and participates in this adjustment to SBTC, involving regulations that are most often a mix of encouragements to stay and work in the host countries along with constraints and legal limitations that render this status a vulnerable one.

Migration and worldwide economic inequality

Relating migration to elementary economic mechanisms shifts the lens beyond the country level. Migration is, in that sense, emblematic of the limitations of restricting the scope to national settings when it comes to studying economic inequality, since economic processes are deeply interrelated and transnational. Analysis of the economic channel by which migration affects inequality dynamics ought to be thought of at a global level; migration as inflows of labor interferes with the global division of labor, with economic implications in national and local labor markets.

Trade economics may seem to be among the most adapted fields to such perspectives. Classical trade theory indeed focuses on the connections between migration, capital and trade. The Hecksher–Ohlin canonical model builds on disparities in countries' relative endowments in the factors of production (labor and capital) to understand patterns of trade of goods and/or people; Stolper and Samuelson's famous model may be regarded as an extension of Hecksher and Ohlin's, with particular attention to the effect of "trade of workers" on wage inequality in host and origin societies (see Samuelson 1948). The Stolper–Samuelson model predicts that, in the context of migration from countries where labor is more abundant, inequality will tend to rise in receiving societies. Refinements of these decisive insights nowadays include sophisticated models with consumption and differential types of goods (Felbermayr et al. 2015). While these models provide theoretical foundations for understanding patterns of movement of labor and its economic effects, the use of countries as the relevant units of analysis is taken for granted, with little consideration given to the power relation between countries and how it shapes movements of people across them. In that sense, while trade economics offers an international framework that helps shed light on the economic mechanisms at stake in labor migration, it tends to conflate the global economy with the international economy.

Research in political economy is more attentive to historically embedded power relations between origin and destination countries/regions. The "international political economy" approach (Massey and Taylor 2004; Mosley and Singer 2015) stresses the growing importance of migration in the current era of globalized capitalism, stimulated by the revolution of means of transport and communication (Castles and Kosack 1973; Sassen 1988; Portes 1997; Castles 2011). Migration is conceived as the "emerging part of the iceberg"; it is in fact one of the manifestations of disparate paces and different intensities of capitalist "advancement" in geographically defined economies (Massey 2009). The increasing mobility of workers, the growing possibility of geographic separation between production and consumption, the rise of multinational productions, etc. are multiple facets of the same general process.

According to this analytical framework, migration reflects the systematic power dynamic between the main components of the global economy. In his *longue durée* historical analyses, Wallerstein (1984) highlights that three structural positions in the global stratification system stabilized around the mid-sixteenth century: the core, the periphery, and the semi-periphery. These positions in the "world-system" translate into differences in state machineries (strong state mechanisms in the core regions and moderate to weak in the peripheral areas) leading to unequal exchanges enforced by strong states on weak ones. Migration may be understood as one among those unequal exchanges.[2] In that sense, migration is the "emerging part of the iceberg" because it is visible in the core (the global North) as a "portion" of the periphery (the global South), and it is characteristic of the exploitation and domination of the latter by the former.

World-system approaches to migration and inequality thus help put the hierarchical dimension of citizenship (and the racial meanings they encapsulate) in perspective and include them among the mechanisms that make migrant labor easier to mobilize and exploit. One might add that world-system theory is particularly compact in this regard, since it directly relates these national hierarchies to the global history of capitalism, which is defined by a unified division of labor taking place in "multiple cultural systems and multiple polities" (Wallerstein 1974). While earlier versions of research on migration within these theoretical perspectives have overwhelmingly focused on South–North migration, contemporary scholarship highlights its explanatory power even when workers move the other way around (from the core to the periphery). Colonial regimes obviously relied on such forms of migration (or settlement) embedded in economic, political, and/or military control (Lucassen and Lucassen 2017). Some aspects of the lives of contemporary Western "expatriates" in former colonies, or more generally in the global South, also involve forms of multifaceted postcolonial domination. These power relations embedded in migration needn't be understood exclusively in terms of state or regional relations: authors such as Sassen (1988) highlight that global cities today concentrate the most advanced forms of capitalism while hosting massive, diverse migratory flows. The particularly polarized nature of migration to global cities that function like "hubs," where high-skilled "cosmopolitan" elites, mainly originating from the global North, meet the service and care workers that overwhelmingly originate from the global South, is particularly emblematic of the embeddedness of this origin-based hierarchy of workers in the division of labor. Global cities represent in this regard the incorporation of portions of "the peripheral areas" into the global networks that channel production, information, and innovation in the global capitalist economy.

Migration Effects on Labor Market Inequality

These theoretical insights that disentangle an economic channel clearly suggest that migration is capable of reshaping inequality in the labor market. First, it is noteworthy that, from a descriptive point of view, migration contributes to overall economic inequality in most Western societies through compositional effects. This contribution is "mechanical" and is basically related to the demographics of migration; in most immigration countries migration tends to concentrate at the bottom of the distribution of income and/or fill up positions at both the top and bottom extremes. In both cases, the compositional effect of migration would thus increase the variance in the overall distribution of income. According to Blau and Kahn (2015), the overall compositional effect of migration on wage inequality is low in the United States. These small compositional effects may nonetheless become more significant if one considers their medium- to long-term contribution to inequality trends. Card (2009) shows that migration accounted for 5 percent of the rise in overall US wage inequality between 1980 and 2000. The main empirical question that the literature tries to tackle is whether, beyond this descriptive (or compositional) associ-ation, migration has a causal effect on the configuration of socioeconomic inequality in the host society. While classic approaches in labor economics have been mostly concerned with the causal effects of migration on natives' labor market outcomes, recent scholarship is also attentive to the ways in which migration is capable of reconfiguring economic inequality within the migrant population and along the gender dimension.

Migration effects on native outcomes

While global approaches to migration and economic inequality mostly focus on the demand side, micro approaches in labor economics pay specific attention to the consequences of migration conceived as an additional supply of workers in the labor market. Borjas's canonical analysis of the "economics of migration" offers a general theoretical framework that relates theories of migration, on the one hand (the wage gap being the main determinant considered), and the ways in which local labor markets adjust to the "shock" of a migrant worker supply, on the other (1989, 1994, 1999). This field of research has specifically inquired into the effect of migration on natives' outcomes (wages and employment). In this respect, it addresses central political concerns, massively mobilized in anti-immigration discourse, about whether migration puts a check on natives' employment chances and decreases their wages.[3] Although Borjas's theoretical framework predicts that migration depresses the cost of labor, the magnitude of its expected effects and their heterogeneity across native worker skill groups are a matter of empirical validity. This gave rise to a rich literature that uses sophisticated identification strategies to disentangle migration's "causal" effect on the wages and employment of natives. Borjas's (2003) own empirical estimates tend to identify quite sizeable negative effects on low-skilled native workers. These findings are nonetheless highly controversial (see, for instance, review of Borjas's 2014 book by Card and Peri 2016). As a matter of fact, nowadays the take-home message of this literature is complex to grasp (Longhi et al. 2010; Ottaviano and Peri 2012; Dustmann et al. 2016). Yet there is a certain consensus that even when negative, overall effects tend to be small (Blau and Kahn 2015; Peri 2016). Card's (1990) influential paper on the Mariel boatlift migration from Cuba to Miami in 1980 – which concludes that there are no significant causal effects – is overwhelmingly cited as a powerful empirical demonstration building on a natural experiment design. This empirical finding might nonetheless vary across contexts and over time, depending on the magnitude and durability of migration, on the one hand, and the economic and political mechanisms adjusting to migratory shocks, on the other. Hunt's (1992) study on the return-colonial migration from Algeria to France, designed in a quite similar fashion to Card's, has, for instance, estimated negative (yet small) effects. According to Hatton, long-term analysis that combines the movements of people and capital is more consistent with negative findings. Drawing on the example of the great migration from

Europe to the "new world" at the turn of the twentieth century, he asserts that it is because migration started affecting natives' wages that immigration states began regulating (and limiting) migration flows. Still, Hatton recognizes that the institutional and demographic contexts of migration are sharply different today. Building on Card (2009), Peri and colleagues criticize the hypothesis, central to Borjas's model, of a perfect substitution between migrant and native workers (Ottaviano and Peri 2012). In their estimates on current migration data in European societies, they conclude that there are small but positive effects and they relate their findings to evidence of imperfect substitution between native and immigrant workers in the same skilled category (Ottaviano and Peri 2006). Natives tend to specialize in communication-intensive occupations, while migrants focus on manual occupations. Using data on 15 European countries, D'Amuri and Peri (2014) also document how immigrants, by taking manual routine jobs, upgrade natives' jobs, giving rise to wage gain for them. Finally, while most of these studies focus on low-skilled natives, recent research increasingly stresses that the effect of migration should be assessed on the entire distribution of wages within native labor. In the United Kingdom, Dustmann and colleagues (2013) measure disparate outcomes of migration at the bottom of the skill distribution (negative effects) in comparison to the rest of the distribution (positive effects). In the United States, Lin and Weiss (2019) have attempted to measure cross-skill effects of migration on native wages. Their results show that there is some evidence of a small negative effect of low-skilled migration on low-skilled native wages; conversely, high-skilled natives seem to benefit both from low-skilled and high-skilled migration. These results point to the fact that low-skilled immigrants compete with the natives at the lower end of the wage distribution but complement the natives in the upper half. High-skilled immigrants, on the other hand, complement both low- and high-skilled natives, but the positive impact is much greater for the latter.[4] Overall, these disparate effects of low- and high-skilled migrant labor across native wage distribution tend to exacerbate wage inequality among natives. According to Dustmann et al. (2013), the evidence that migration increases wage inequality at the bottom of the distribution derives from the fact that migrants are remunerated below the marginal productivity level, which allows native workers (particularly the high-skilled among them) to share a "surplus"; in other terms, migrant labor is more exploitable by firms, which also means that immigration re-evaluates native labor. Evidence of the overqualification of migrants hints at similar mechanisms of exploitation and re-evaluation of native labor: the proportion of migrants with tertiary-level education in low- and medium-skilled occupations is considerably larger than that of natives (the gap is around 12 percentage points in OECD countries – OECD 2018: 94).

It is noteworthy that these approaches to the effect of migration on "domestic economies" have been generalized beyond the strict analysis of labor market outcomes. Migration impact assessments comprise growth and real income per capita, international trade, foreign investment, innovation and entrepreneurship, housing prices and the housing market, spatial segregation, as well as trust and social cohesion (Nijkamp et al. 2012).

Migration, women, and minorities in the labor market

Most of the studies reviewed above tend to measure the effect of migration in terms of natives' outcomes, arguably with the aim of bringing some empirical evidence to the often-heated political debate on the economic costs/benefits of migration. Nonetheless, and somewhat paradoxically, despite considerable variability in the theoretical approaches and a wide range of nuances in the findings, migrant labor's effects on natives' outcomes tend to be small, if any. Conversely, there is considerable evidence that new migration does affect labor market positions of earlier migrants and, more generally, ethnic/racial minority populations. Empirical assessments relating to the ways in which migration has been reshaping the socioeconomic position of women in the labor market are also more and more conclusive. In brief, rather than affecting the situation of natives in particular, migration seems capable of transforming categorical hierarchies that organize the labor market.

From the economic theory perspective, migrant labor is most likely to affect employment and wages of workers who are the most substitutable with recently arrived flows. Borjas's canonical framework (1987, 1994) already suggested that older migrant and ethnoracial minority workers may be the most affected by labor market effect of recent migration. In the United States in particular, there is a well-established tradition of labor market analysis that focuses on migration impact in terms of displacing/replacing African Americans in the job markets. In his seminal work on New York City, which combines the use of 1940–90 census data as well as ethnographic research, Waldinger (1996) sketches a thorough analysis of the local labor market, in which native white, native black, and immigrant workers' behaviors and outcomes are closely related. While Waldinger's approach is not causal, and he is quite cautious about claiming that migrants displaced African Americans (he actually shows that this is not the case), his perspective was among the first to factor in both structural labor market opportunities (vacancies in the manufacturing industry mostly created by white suburbanization, levels of anti-black hiring discrimination in the private sector) and also labor market expectations of minority and migrant workers and their perception of what is a good or a bad job. While African Americans' rising aspirations in the context of the post-civil rights era pushes them to avoid persisting discrimination in industries, instead preferring the public sector, migrants are far more willing to accept job slots at the bottom of the job hierarchy, which allows them to enter key industries and develop ethnic niches within them. Through network effects and the development of a business oriented social capital, these niches then act as self-generating processes, enhancing migrants' employability and their relative economic success in comparison to native minorities. A few years after Waldinger's study, Bean and Bell-Rose (1999) published a book that provides an overview of the effects of postwar migration on economic and spatial dynamics that exert specific concerns toward the potential detrimental impacts of migrant labor on ethnic minorities in general and African Americans in particular. And today, even the more standardized causal assessments of the effects of migration, particularly within the economic literature, do show that its impacts tend to be most substantial when the focus is on the outcomes of "old immigrants" and on ethnoracial minorities.

Interpretations of these findings sometimes stress the high competition at the lowest end of the labor market, where migrants are very likely to encounter earlier migrants and/or native minority labor. Nonetheless, recent research at the intersection of sociology, economics, and industrial relations highlights the idea that these mechanisms of displacement/replacement are more generally related to the categorical feature of the organization of most labor markets. There is indeed a lot of evidence on occupational sorting, niches, and typification of tasks that suggests that particular jobs are matched to categorically distinctive workers (Tomaskovic-Devey 2014). Gender, nationality, ethnicity, race, and other categorical divisions are powerful in mediating access to occupations and positions. Although a considerable share of the explanatory mechanisms is strongly related to the ways in which social norms shape preferences (what job seekers consider to be the most desirable jobs for them), research on the hiring behaviors of employers also convincingly documents their role in this categorical matching of jobs to subpopulations. Although current evidence on employers' direct taste-based discrimination in hiring is clear and convincing, it is true that employers also discriminate "statistically" because of widespread beliefs that categorical distinctions correlate well with hidden labor-relevant factors such as productivity, motivations, effort, etc. And discrimination in the form of "barriers" and denial of access to opportunities is only one aspect of the picture. More generally, these differential tastes and beliefs also trigger the steering and channeling of workers into sectors, types of jobs, and positions. Ethnographic research documents how, in their search for the most "appropriate workers," employers rely on categorically framed "suitability," in terms of gender but also in terms of migratory/ethnic/racial criteria that they argue are informative when it comes to labor-relevant worker attributes (Neckerman and Kirschenman 1991; Waldinger and Lichter 2003; Ruhs and Anderson 2012). It is the conjunction of the desirability of jobs within some groups with this categorical typification of the preferences and behaviors of employers that produces systematic biases in the distribution of jobs, occupations, and positions and the rewards that are associated with them. The arrival of "new migrants" as job seekers is capable of affecting this categorical organization of the labor market. Evidence suggests that the rescaling of typical "old minority" and/or "native" occupations is a common mechanism; new migrants tend to fill the lower level of the occupational hierarchy, pushing earlier migrants, minorities, and natives up the occupational ladder. But other organizational mechanisms may also be at stake. Some are related to the transformation of power relations within the workplace (Tomaskovic-Devey et al. 2015; Melzer et al. 2018). Migrant communities may also engage in a parallel organization of the labor market, creating alternative business or occupational niches (Eckstein and Peri 2018). And preferences and aspirations of native minorities are sometimes confronted with the reality of long-lasting discrimination that blocks their ability to progress because of the arrival of new migrants at the bottom end of the labor market.

These perspectives shift the lens to the relational mechanisms at stake in labor market-based resource distribution processes. Recent developments in relational inequality theory specifically focus on the ways in which categorical distinctions are intensified or muted by the intersection of individual, organizational, and institutional contexts, among which industries, sectors, and workplaces are central (other important settings are neighborhoods, cities, countries, schools, etc.) (Tomaskovic-Devey and Avent-Holt 2019). This context-specific approach to the division of labor is more conducive to open-ended outcomes in the labor market and different effects on different categories of workers (DiTomaso et al. 2007).

Beyond the division of paid labor, migration is also a source of adjustment in the intrinsic tensions between paid and unpaid labor in capitalist economies, a tension that also tends to be solved through categorical divisions. The increasing participation of women in the labor market in many industrialized societies over recent decades has been accompanied by a growing reliance on "female migrant work" channeled to fulfill the shortage of labor provoked by the withdrawal of "native" women, mainly in what is referred to as the "care service" (Anderson 2000). Nonetheless, while the congruence in the timing of increased female migration and a higher participation rate of women in migration societies is clear, the causality between migration trends and women's behavior in the labor market is difficult to disentangle. Research shows that migration reduces the prices of services such as childcare, housekeeping, and elderly care, which in turn affects the labor supply of women, specifically those who are highly skilled (Barone and Mocetti 2011). In an attempt to document these mechanisms at the micro level, Cortés and Tessada (2011) have, for instance, delved into the relation between low-skilled migration and the increase in hours of paid work for highly educated American women and the decrease of hours spent on household work. While cultural shifts, the transformation of gender norms, and the increasing gender egalitarian legal framework are often seen as the driving forces of the female conquest of the labor market and the overall improvement of their economic well-being in developed societies, migration definitely plays a part – albeit one that is often hidden – of the female economic emancipation story. But even as migrant labor made native women's entry into the labor market possible, or at least easier – thus reconfiguring gender inequality in host societies – it has at the same time been driving inequality among females, widening the gap between highly and low-educated women. In other words, women's participation in the paid sector was made possible through the transfer of a considerable share of formerly unpaid female work to less-educated migrant women in the form of low-paid jobs (rather than through a more even allocation between men and women). If one adds the ethnoracial dimension to the picture – with the overt racialization of household and care work – the feminization of the workforce offers a highly intersectional case for the study of the relation between migration and inequality. And here again, female migration provides the type of work, household and care work, that meets the needs of the division of labor. These massive changes in the gendered feature of migration have been increasingly exposing female migrants to specific forms of economic vulnerability that are quite different from the ones experienced by male migrants. They also tend to sharpen labor market differences within the female migrant population in terms of legal status, as family reunion migrant women are traditionally characterized by their low level of participation in the labor market (Lersch 2015; Vickstrom and González-Ferrer 2016). Research also suggests that this increasing income-earning role of female migrants may enhance women's power within immigrant households, thereby reshaping marital and family relations (Mills 2003; Farris 2012).

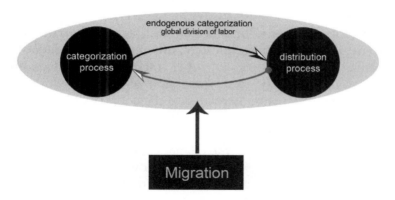

Figure 3.1 Migration and inequality: the economic channel

All in all, and despite fundamental differences between the theoretical and the empirical approaches, this prolific interdisciplinary literature focuses on labor-related mechanisms as the main channel through which migration affects social inequality. Figure 3.1 attempts to represent this channel. The global division of labor and the resource distribution that stems from it endogenously construct "migrants" as a category of workers. The migration and global division of labor nexus shifts the analysis of economic inequality, and labor market dynamics in particular, toward transnational perspectives. In a sort of extension of the classical analysis of the role of the division of labor in social stratification regimes, portrayed as the process generating both the unequal distribution of resources and the unequal social categories that emanate from it, the global division of labor approach highlights the ways in which migration shapes categorizations that are grounded in the unequal distribution of jobs, positions, and economic rewards worldwide. Hence, it is not only the division of labor that becomes global in this framework; also the class structure that arises from it is a global/transnational class structure. In other words, migration provides types of labor, and migrants become types of workers (Anderson 2010). While the economics literature puts forward some macroeconomic factors (barriers to trade, differences in technology, differences in the endowments of workers or in other factors of production between countries), this typification of migrant work is also shown to be simply related to the country of location. Using a natural experiment building on randomized visa processing in the United States, Clemens (2010) compares wages of workers in the same firms using the same technology and finds that location outside India causes a six-fold increase in the wages and that only a small portion of this earnings gap can be attributed to worker traits of any kind or to differences in the technology of production. These results hint at the extent to which a worker's country of location nominally determines his or her labor rewards.

Nonetheless, despite the centrality of the approach in terms of "global social class," the literature that links migration and labor market inequality tends to be increasingly intersectional. The economic channel is relevant not only to understanding inequality between migrant and native workers; it also affects inequalities within natives (the high-skilled versus the low-skilled; female versus male workers; majority versus minority workers) and within migrants (between old and new migrants, along ethnic/racial lines) (Phillips and Massey 1999).

Migration and the Economic Channel of Inequality: The Complexity of the Underlying Factors

Some criticism tends to put the centrality of the economic channel into perspective, highlighting the steady decrease in the labor component of contemporary migration. For example, only one-third of migrants to the European Union are "official" labor migrants (OECD and EU 2016: 13). Migration flows are increasingly composed of family reunions, students, retirees, refugees, and other "humanitarian" categories, including environmental ones. This criticism is actually hardly justifiable, since the distinction between economic and non-economic migrants is largely constructed by current migration policies in the context of harshening border controls. While surveys show that people leave their homeland for various reasons, the fact is that migrants are predominantly of working age; thus, they ultimately add to the workforce in destination countries. It is clear, therefore, that, although their migration was related to wars and violence, particularly in the Middle East, recent flows of refugees and asylum seekers raise questions regarding their access to the labor market. For example, the OECD–UNHCR action plan, "Engaging with Employers in the Hiring of Refugees," shows that policy actions in terms of migrant employability is at stake even for "officially" non-economic migration. Regardless of the central motivation that pushes people to migrate, migrants ultimately and overwhelmingly get to search for jobs and participate in the labor market. And even when direct labor recruitment becomes less prominent in driving migration, social networks, migration chains, and other mechanisms of cumulative causation are decisive in creating the demand for additional migration in which labor is a central component.

Moreover, and perhaps more fundamentally, this criticism tends to overlook the fact that the organized "import" of labor migration, whether state- and/or business-monitored, is still operating in many parts of the world, especially for migration in Southern countries (Skeldon 2000; Sassen 2008). And even within Western countries, a close look at certain economic sectors clearly hints at the centrality of migration in organizing the labor market; services to buildings and landscape activities, residential care activities, warehousing and support activities for transportation, and manufacturing of food products are all industries with the largest changes in employment by place of birth in OECD countries over the 2012–17 period (OECD 2018: 92). Consequently, and despite important acknowledgments of multidimensional driving factors (demographic, political, ecological, cultural, etc.), labor migration is still at the foreground of the picture.

Another common criticism pertains to the prevalence of the economic channel in explaining migrants' position in the labor market. The problem is related to the fact that, when it comes to migrants' socioeconomic outcomes, empirical studies often end up distinguishing in their findings amongst origin-based (or ethnoracial) categories of migrants. These distinctions sometimes rely on country-level classification, but they also often utilize wide categorical groupings, such as "Western" immigrants, "EU/non-EU" immigrants, "Muslim" immigrants. This ethnoracial categorization (which will be at the center of the discussion in Chapter 5) is "external" to the labor market and hints at the drawbacks of a homogenizing vision of migrants' positions within it.

There are nonetheless some theoretical attempts that try to incorporate this heterogeneity of migrants' economic outcomes along ethnoracial lines into a unified migration-driven analytical framework. The concept of assimilation is one of the most successful in doing so. Differential gaps in employment and wages tend to be interpreted as reflecting a range of temporary maladjustments (linguistic, cultural, educational, etc.), the levels of which vary across immigrant origins. This approach thus portrays migrant trajectories as a form of progressive adjustment. Earlier migration economists somehow endorsed – quite unusually, one might add – these originally sociological perspectives in the context of their own theoretical elaborations on the concept of human capital. Chiswick (1978), for example, pioneered the study of immigrant labor market assimilation in economics, highly influenced by the emerging "new labor economics" that focuses on human capital investment in the prediction of economic outcomes – for instance in Mincer's (1958) and Becker's (1964) theoretical contributions. These sociological and economic perspectives share a taste for an overarching theoretical framework capable of accounting for the situation of all migrants, despite their heterogeneity, in the labor market in particular, but also in society in general. As a prominent migration economist puts it, Park's 1928 model of the "marginal man" is a "single process that applies to all immigrants, culminating in their cultural and economic assimilation" (Duleep 2015: 108).

Nonetheless, empirical studies document large gaps in immigrant and native labor market outcomes (employment, occupations, wages) in most societies, with consistent and durable variations along migrant subgroups. These gaps are hardly reducible to "adjustment" issues, whether economic or cultural, since they tend to persist despite long residency. These gaps hint at mechanisms of discrimination that are related not necessarily only to migrant labor in itself, but also to specific origins, phenotypes, or cultural attributes within migrant subpopulations. Although disentangling the migratory from the ethnoracial is quite complex (Adida et al. 2016), some pair audit studies have managed to assess that, within migrants, it is these attributes that explain unequal access to jobs. Valfort (2017) has shown, for instance, that "anti-Muslim" discrimination in the French labor market explains differential access to employment of Muslim/ non-Muslim migrants coming from the same country of origin (namely Lebanon).

Things become even more complicated when it comes to migrants' descendants, who, having been born, socialized, educated, and trained in the host society, are not, strictly speaking, an imported labor force. Many of them still nonetheless experience sizeable socioeconomic gaps, again with a great deal of variation across parental origin (OECD 2017). In other words, beyond the idea of the typification of migrant work, which is central to the economic channel exposed in this chapter, there is a need to address the ways in which categorization of migrant workers is produced and understood and the prevalence that is conferred upon it. One central underlying issue is the extent to which the migrant/native worker category is a pure "socioeconomic construction" (stemming from the hardcore economic mechanisms driving the global division of labor) or whether it is susceptible to interaction with other categorizations, namely the ethnoracial ones, embedding them further in labor market mechanisms (Solomos and Wrench 1995; Wrench et al. 1999).

The most simplified versions within Marxian and neo-Marxian perspectives on migrant labor tend to see categorization processes involved in migrant labor as a "conspiracy of capitalists" that serves to divide the working class. In that sense, the migrant type of worker is a pure "construction," which serves the interest of capital in nationally framed capitalist economies that are, in reality, transnational.[5] Contrary to this hard socio-economic constructivism of migrant labor, Piore (1979) conducts an analysis of dualism in the labor market that leaves more room for migrants' agency, arguing that some workers (migrants and women in particular) may happen to be less reluctant than others to occupy positions in the secondary labor market. Migrants may indeed be less "geographically attached" to the labor market, and they may have plans of return or re-migration, which makes their acceptance of these positions temporary (Doeringer and Piore 1971). Piore emphasizes similarities between "domestic" and "foreign" migration, pointing out that employers "find" these "categories of workers" that fit the secondary labor market at least partly for "accidental reasons" and use them in the "institutional arrangements" that organize labor market dualism. This framework helps clarify the historical role of employers in facilitating migrant labor despite growing "nationalist" anti-immigration attitudes. Nonetheless, at least two "less accidental" factors also explain the propensity of migrants to occupy these disadvantaged labor market positions: the first is economic, the second is symbolic. On the economic side, path-dependency in world-system inequality translates into systematic gaps in both the quality of jobs and the quantity of associated rewards, which pushes migrants from the most disadvantaged countries to accept positions that, although relatively unfavorable in the host country, still appear advantageous in comparison with their origin country's labor conditions. It is thus their "structural position" within two unequal labor markets that opens up this "bind of freedom" on which dualist labor market arrangements in host societies build. Ethnographic research describes how employers elaborate on this narrative when justifying the clustering of immigrant workers in low-end positions, invoking the wages of misery they might have earned in their home countries (Waldinger and Lichter 2003; Matthews and Ruhs 2007). From a symbolic point of view, the hierarchical dimension of citizenship triggers the propensity of migrants to accept "subordinate" labor positions, interiorizing their symbolic status as "subordinate-country citizens" or even more generally as "subordinate racial/ethnic group members" (Castles 2005). Symbolic mechanisms are also at stake when it comes to the rationales of employer behaviors; relying on an ethnographic research on Wisconsin dairy farms, Harrison and Lloyd (2013) emphasize the complex array of reasons for which employers cluster immigrants in low-end positions (to maintain profits, meet their own middle-class aspirations, manage their concerns on immigration policy, assert their class identity, maintain their privileges, etc.). One may argue that these two "less accidental" factors that sort migrants on economic/symbolic grounds necessitate powerful, taken-for-granted social constructions that separate migrants from natives, but also distinguish subcategories of migrants. Ethnoracial categorization processes, including nation-state building, have been doing this for the last two centuries (see Chapter 5 for more details). The example of the European Union, and its attempts to create a unified labor market through the establishment of free intra-EU movement of people, provides clear insights into this sociopolitical construction underlying the migrant type of labor (and the possibility of deconstructing it). This entails changes in language and terminology as Europe increasingly uses the concept of mobility rather than migration to refer to those workers who cross national boundaries within the EU (Favell 2008; Rea 2013; Recchi 2015).

On the other hand, and contrary to the overly simplified versions of migrant labor that tend to represent migrant workers as "victims" of global economic forces and interests, contemporary empirical studies stress migrants' agency and their capacity to reshape labor and employment conditions. Research on employer–employee bargaining power is interesting in this regard; while migrant workers portrayed as vulnerable and (consequently) docile are supposed to weaken workers' bargaining power, another potential mechanism consists in migration's changing the factor endowment of the economy and therefore the balance in bargaining power between capital and labor. This renders the relation between migration and labor empowerment more complex. Moreover, the new economics of labor migration stresses the fact that international migrants are not only workers in the global economy, but also risk-minimizers seeking to cope with failures in insurance and credit markets at home (Stark 1991). Migration is thus partly aiming at repatriating earnings in transnational households. This literature draws attention to the fact that migrants are not merely imported work, they are also senders of capital. The important role played by remittances in the global economy should also be incorporated into the economic channel.

In conclusion, the economic channel is central to our understanding of the relation between migration and inequality dynamics. It offers a powerful framework that helps us understand the endogeneity of the categorization of migrants as types of workers within the global division of labor. In addition to shifting the lens of standard analyses of socioeconomic inequality in the social stratification literature toward a transnational and global perspective, the economic channel also draws attention to the need to take into account the myriad of protagonists involved in the "migration industry"; this means migrants themselves, of course, but also states, firms, professional branches, unions, and more.

— 4 —

The Legal Channel: Immigration Law, Administrative Management of Migrants, and Civic Stratification

This chapter elaborates on the legal channel through which migration affects inequality. In Chapter 1, I discussed the limitations of defining migration only in relation to geographic mobility, highlighting its linkage with the relatively recent institutionalization of community borders in the form of nation-state membership. This chapter is dedicated to the transformation of political membership brought about by migration and its consequences in terms of inequality. Political membership refers here to formal affiliation with a political community, implying legal codification, institutionalization, and official documentation, with tangible consequences in terms of rights and political status.

In the relation between migration and inequality, the legal channel pertains to the ways in which migration interferes with the codification of modern citizenship, understood as encompassing the wide and stratified spectrum of individual relations and affiliations to the state. While C. Joppke (2010) distinguishes, in his seminal contribution, three dimensions of citizenship – status, rights, and identity[1] – I choose to deal with the identity dimension separately, because its relation to social inequality implies different dynamics, which I will develop in the next chapter. This chapter, therefore, is primarily concerned with the relation between migration and the first two dimensions of citizenship. Status and rights are shaped by legal norms that uncover a particular nexus in the relation between migration and inequality. As a consequence of the current "world polity" organizational context that systematically classifies the planet's inhabitants as nation-state citizens (Meyer et al. 1997), contemporary migration gives rise to legal and administrative processes of human categorization that establish a continuum of membership positions, or "ranks," within immigration countries. In other words, this chapter is concerned with the consequences of migration on inequality that are channeled through the formal link to the *state*, while the relationship to the *nation* is covered with the ethnic and racial dimensions in the next chapter.

Migration, Citizenship, and Legal Categorization

As a legally enforced relationship linking individuals to states, citizenship can be understood as a sorting system that overwhelmingly relies on birthplace characteristics (individual or parental, or a combination of the two). There is a fundamental tension in the modern conceptualization of citizenship; while it tends to be associated with the achievement of formal equality *within* nation-states, which supposedly positively spills over into political, economic, and social equality (Marshall 1950), it is also de facto one of the most powerful inegalitarian principles of classification *across* nation-states, allocating privilege and disadvantage according to place of birth – a strictly ascriptive attribute (Shachar 2009). Brubaker (1992) famously refers to this tension by differentiating between the external and internal dimensions of citizenship. In his effort to quantify the "citizenship premium/penalty" using individual-level worldwide income data, Milanovic (2016) underscores the contradiction in the principle of equality of opportunity, whether we look within nation-states or between them. International migration renders this double standard of equality flagrant. Migrants transgress the principle of political membership grounded in birthright by seeking residency in a country other than their birthplace, consequently challenging the rigidity and stability of the taken-for-granted system of human classification underlying modern citizenship.[2] Migration, therefore, is situated directly at the cutting edge of citizenship. From the point of view of the receiving country, it entails first and foremost the lack of membership, which is manifest in the use of the term "alien" to describe immigrants. From its very starting point, upon the crossing of state borders, and throughout subsequent settlement and residency, migration brings about series of legally enforced (re)classifications. States rely on a wide range of infrastructures, which may be referred to generally as legal infrastructures, whose fundamental role is to produce, enforce, warrant, and reinforce these classifications with the aim of protecting the boundaries of political membership (Guiraudon and Joppke 2001; Helbling et al. 2017). These infrastructures comprise institutions such as parliaments, criminal justice systems, and police, but also diverse types of bureaucracies, administrations, and public agencies. Some migratory categories also derive from supra-state (international law, European law) or infra-state (diverse forms of regional governance) institutions or involve some interstate agreements. These diverse legal authorities engage in the production of categorizations that take place from the very first moment of border crossing (upon migration) and continue to affect settlement and residency in the host country.

From border control to entry types and legal status

Legal processes for classification upon migration are closely related to border control procedures. They rely on a wide range of "devices" that are constantly being changed and adapted to deal with new situations of migration, and that are strongly dependent on technological conditions. The general contemporary trend has nonetheless been toward harsher and more selective border control procedures. Before the 1920s, major receiving countries raised few barriers to entries and most sending societies had limited means to control emigration (Martín 2008; Abramitzky et al. 2012). At the inspection station of New York's Ellis Island, the processing system for the most massive migration in human history was extremely rapid – about two hours, which was mainly spent taking photos, registering identities, and sometimes performing medical checks. It was also non-selective, at least on socio-economic grounds; selection mostly occurred during the migration process as migrants had to cross the Atlantic and survive the hardship of what was, at that time, a hard journey. In the current age of global transportation and worldwide connectivity, the incongruence between the porosity of physical/geographic borders and the rigidity of political borders becomes more and more salient (Torpey 1999). Contemporary technologies of border control are extremely rigorous: they involve a wide array of tools, ranging from the administrative (passports, visas, permits, etc.) to the heavily military (checkpoints, border fortification, construction and security surveillance of fences and walls, maritime surveillance, etc.) and the biomedical (individual identity control relying on phenotypical, biometric, and biological attributes including DNA-based identification) (Fassin and D'halluin 2005; Lakhani and Timmermans 2014). Border control is not merely about entry processing; it also involves apprehensions within the receiving country, detention and deportation (Meissner et al. 2013, Rosenblum and Meissner 2014, Wong 2015). The legitimacy of state control on geographical mobility gained ground throughout the twentieth century, leading to the generalization of migratory restrictions.

Migration control is also an issue for the sending societies. While the enforcement of emigration restriction regulation might turn out to be quite complex, many sending states, such as the Philippines, Brazil, Morocco, and Mexico, to give a few examples, have been increasingly implementing programs to manage their outflows, facilitating certain types of migration, and enhancing economic, political, and symbolic relations to their diaspora (FitzGerald 2006; Levitt and de la Dehesa 2010; Lee 2017). More generally, the emigration/immigration nexus actually creates a "field" in which interdependent state administrations participate in establishing migration control routines, thus influencing both the volume and the direction of migration. Moreover, migration control procedures are dragged into international relations: agreements, tensions, conflicts, and diverse forms of interstate power relations play important roles in shaping population movements across countries (Thiollet 2011). Some prior colonialist relations have, for instance, transformed into a form of "remote control" with ex-colonizer states regulating postcolonial migration at the point of origin (Sayad 1999; Zolberg 2008). This intertwining of migration control with geopolitics can be seen in the current management of the so-called "migration crisis," which increasingly entails extraterritorial surveillance, thus calling into question the definition of state borders in international law (Menjivar 2014). Indeed, the European Union has been seeking to enforce an overarching system of surveillance of the Mediterranean, pushing its effective borders to maritime space or "externalizing" border management to the sovereign space of non-European countries that have been transformed into "buffer states" (as shown in the EU–Turkey deal in the context of the "migrant crisis," or through the creation of "hotspots" in sub-Saharan African countries) (De Wenden et al. 2015; Schmoll and Tahir 2018).

All in all, whether emanating directly from the state or from local or global institutions, the legitimacy and ability to control migration is closely related to the gradual construction of an organizational legal framework and the building of the administrative infrastructure that goes with it. The process of legal state-building inevitably led to increasing legal codification of migration all across states, regardless of their heterogeneity. In the case of the European Union, the process of legally codifying diverse forms of migration and establishing the administrations, agencies, and bureaucracies required for such a process has been relatively sporadic, mainly due to a lack of constraints and weak political coordination between EU member states on this issue. This led to successive dynamics of first creating and then dismantling agencies that enforce EU agreements on external frontier control and surveillance (Guiraudon 2003).

Spending dedicated to the enforcement of "immigration and national security" policies is considerable and has been steadily increasing in most modern democracies (Meissner et al. 2013).[3] It is nonetheless noteworthy that, given the financial, administrative, and military means it demands, migration regulation is particularly enforced in countries where the government has the economic means and the political power to control entry and enforce deportation. This is not the case in "weak" states, in which the boundaries of citizenship are consequently more open (Sadiq 2008). Also, migrant controls are more or less strict depending on the origins of migrants: most Western citizens can enter virtually all the world's states with few or no constraints and regulations, whereas obtaining a visa, even for a single visit, is rapidly becoming mission impossible for citizens of the global South countries. This reality hints at the geopolitics of migration control.

One of the most influential legal categorizations driven by migration, and surely the most straightforward, relies on a basic criterion of legality of entry. Entering with or without legal approval automatically creates two categories of migrants: legal migrants on the one hand, and what are variably called illegal, undocumented, unauthorized, or unlawful migrants on the other. The administrative process of migration categorization automatically formulates unauthorized migration as "outside the law" (Motomura 2014) by distinguishing, among the de facto residents, between those for whom access is "accepted" and those for whom it is "denied."[4] Aside from this dichotomous categorization, migration management also creates "inside the law" entry-type categorizations distinguishing among visitors, labor migrants, seasonal or temporary workers, students, family reunion migrants, accompanying spouses, asylum seekers, etc. This wide spectrum of categories shows that the boundary separating insiders and outsiders is more blurred than it might appear. And even within individual lives, legality and illegality interfere in immigrant biographies (Jasso 2011; Menjívar and Abrego 2012; Chauvin et al. 2013).

These aspects of entry management produce a series of migration-related legal and administrative categories. At the state level, these categories derive from a combination of more or less harmonized policies: interior and security, foreign affairs, employment, urban, and sometimes those specific to immigration. While most of these categorizations have been produced and enforced by nation-states, international laws, European laws, federal laws, or other entities of legal categorization also affect the definition of migrant legal status. This is the case for the "refugee" category, which stems from international law and is used today, albeit with considerable variation in terms of conditions and requirements, in most state-level administrative categorizations of migrants. Another example is how the creation of the European Union led to the implementation of a variety of mobility categories for EU and non-EU residents (i.e., free movement migration, the EU Blue Card, seasonal workers, posted workers, etc.) (Berezin and Schain 2004; Favell 2008; Recchi 2015).[5] This proliferation of mobility categorization inevitably instills a form of stratification of European citizenship (Kofman 2002; Recchi 2016).

These legal and administrative categories are highly dependent on migration contexts and conditions. As a consequence, they keep changing; some disappear and others emerge in response to specific situations of migration or in relation to governmental and institutional changes. During the recent "refugee crisis," Germany created a new legal category, "*Bleibeperspektive*," which literally means "prospect of staying," in order to lessen traditional restrictions of labor market access to refugees and facilitate the integration of the massive arrival of migrant populations (Vetters 2017; Meissner 2018). Since 2016, the British vote to exit the European Union has been driving a fundamental restructuring of immigration administration and management in the United Kingdom, ending the free movement of EU citizens and changing several aspects of the administrative process both for new and established migrants (McGhee et al. 2017).

Citizenship and immigration laws

Legal migratory categorization doesn't stop at the border: it continues to affect the lives of migrants and their descendants during their residency in the destination country. Most of this continuing categorization derives from citizenship and immigration laws, with the effect of stratifying membership in the host society. Citizenship law defines the rules of allocation of membership, its transmission across generations, and the conditions under which it could be revoked. From this perspective, migrants can be regarded as "citizens in waiting" (Motomura 2007). They are more or less so depending on the extent to which this categorical transition (the passage from alien to citizen) is encouraged and facilitated. Classical approaches in political sciences and history have highlighted the distinction between *jus soli* and *jus sanguinis* and the

ways in which this reflects different "philosophies" of
citizenship and distinct models of immigrant integration
(Brubaker 2001; Favell 2001). In the meantime, as
non-citizen residents, these migrant "citizens in waiting"
are subject to laws and regulations that apply to "aliens"
or "foreigners" covering a wide range of issues, such
as work authorization, geographic localization, electoral
participation, access to public services, access to welfare,
taxation, etc.

A prolific literature describes the ways in which
citizenship law has been shaping migrants' integration
in host societies and how it gets affected in turn by
migration trends (Bloemraad et al. 2008). According
to Joppke (2010), a certain process of convergence of
citizenship, at least within "liberal democracies," is clearly
related to immigration patterns and trends. The recent
change in German nationality law, introducing some *jus
soli* components in a country that has long been presented
as the prototype of differentialist citizenry, provides one
of the most striking examples. The greater tolerance
for dual or multiple nationalities in both emigration
and immigration countries points to similar dynamics
induced by migration (Faist and Kivisto 2007; Sejersen
2008; Bauböck 2010). Scholars have nonetheless been
putting into perspective this convergence toward a more
liberal apprehension of citizenship, and the most recent
events seem to support their skepticism. In the United
States, the stigmatization of sustained immigration has
reinforced demands for a more exclusivist framing of
citizenship. Similar dynamics have been observed in Spain
(Martín-Pérez and Moreno-Fuentes 2012). Even more
radically, migration states in the Gulf region have been
reacting to their growing dependency on migrant labor
by reinforcing the exclusivity of their citizenship (Joppke
2017). While numerous recent examples tend to discredit
the "postnational" conjuncture, the fact that migration
is locally transforming the very contours of the definition
of the "national" through changes in citizenship law is

beyond doubt, though there is a fair amount of variation in the direction these transformations are taking. The vast output from the social sciences on transnationalism has traditionally been analyzing the challenges posed by migration to the territorial and monolithic apprehension of citizenship. Migration in effect creates situations of multiple state affiliations, calling into question the understanding of citizenship as membership to the state in which one lives. While these challenges to the territorial dimension of citizenship are perceptible in both sending and receiving countries, migrants' transnational lives are still very much shaped by their relationships to these two states (Waldinger 2015; Green and Waldinger 2016).

In a similar vein to nationality and formal political affiliation, alien laws are specifically designed to manage migration and have been changing in relation to the latter's patterns and trends. In the late 1990s, scholars emphasized the emergence of the status of denizens in an attempt to denote a certain decoupling of civic and social rights from formal citizenship. This trend was supposed to be particularly intense in Europe, where birthright citizenship has traditionally been rather rare, while, as a consequence of continual migration, a significant portion of the population consists of communities that reside permanently in the country without formal membership (Soysal 1994; Yuval-Davis 1997). These questions became all the more pressing as the nature of immigration changed in most European countries, taking less and less often the form of temporary or guest worker migration. Debates over opening space for political participation by foreign nationals, for example by granting them the right to vote in local elections, have emerged in the political agendas of many countries. Migrants form a group of residents who are very much affected by laws, rules, and norms without being included in their decision-making, which runs contrary to the basic political principles of liberal democracies (Dahl 1989; Young 2000). Migration has also been provoking debates on the rights to vote in the homeland countries for "external citizens" or "expats." Transnational approaches are again valuable here, and they stress the increasing importance of consular services in the lives of "emigrants," both in terms of access to the vote and in relation to the provision of different documentation services (Levitt and de la Dehesa 2010; Waldinger 2014). And beyond electoral rights, legal debates on "multicultural and group rights" have also been gaining ground in immigration societies, mainly in relation to the retention of language and religion by migrant communities.

The direction in which these debates have been evolving since the early 2000s is still far from being straightforward (Koopmans et al. 2012). While local and regional membership proved to be more easily extensible, allowing foreigners to vote at local and municipal elections in many countries, the road toward "denizenship" has been considerably slowed down by legal reforms that are harsher and harsher on the foreign nationals. Limiting alien rights, restricting access to nationality while easing its revocation, denying minority rights and status, hardening detention conditions, criminalizing undocumented migration, restricting access to health care, etc.: these are a few examples of the direction alien rights have been taking in many immigration countries, including the most liberal ones such as the Netherlands and Denmark. Political events such as post-9/11 in the United States and post-November 2015 in France may have provoked backlash effects in this regard. Economic crisis, austerity, and the rise of populism probably play an important role as well. These recent trends highlight the constant vulnerability of non-citizens, including in well-established liberal democracies.

In most immigration societies, laws, and the diverse institutions that take part in their production and enforcement, have been functioning as a "migration categorization machine." The dissemination of legal categories of migration occurs through the interaction between social sciences and public policy. While their construction and implementation are overwhelmingly situated in the policy sphere, these categories are used more and more as "knowledge categories." For instance, in its standard publications, the OECD has been increasingly breaking down conventional statistics (labor market outcomes or other types of immigrant integration measurements, residential outcomes, naturalization, etc.) by migration legal categories (mainly referring to entry-type categorization) (see Figure 4.1). The fact that these migratory categories were originally constructed within the state increases their legitimacy and stimulates their depiction as "relevant categories." They are sometimes interpreted as potential measurements of migration motivations or migration causes. This understanding is questionable because there is, in fact, a considerable mismatch between these administratively driven categorizations and their practical meaning in migrants' lives: at the individual level, for example, it is extremely difficult to disentangle whether migration is forced or voluntary, temporary or permanent, motivated by family reunion, work, or study, etc. (Collyer and De Haas 2012). Given the differential in the ability to migrate (along gender, class, family background, national lines, etc.) and the fact that immigration policies apply unevenly across these lines, understanding migration legal categories as intrinsically meaningful "modes of migration" is misleading (Carling and Collins 2018).

It remains true nonetheless that the increasing reliance on categorization and standardization technologies in migration policy is actually dramatically changing the face of immigration in many countries. As shown in recent US research, profound legal transformations have been shifting not only the distribution of immigrants across legal categories (such as naturalized citizens, legal aliens, undocumented aliens, permanent residents, etc.) but also the rewards/penalties associated with these categories. This affects the composition of the immigrant population considerably, thus challenging the stability and consistency of the "immigrant/foreign-born" category in scientific

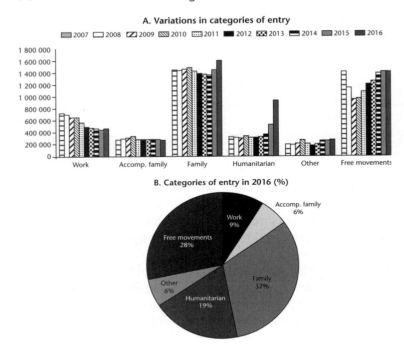

Figure 4.1 Legal and administrative categorization of migration in OECD countries
Source: OECD 2018: 26

research and beyond in public policy (Massey and Bartley 2005).

All in all, whether they are assigned upon migration or later during the settlement process, migratory categories share in common the fact that they are constructed by the law. Thus, migration and the arrival of "new populations" in a formally defined political entity nominally increase legally enforced categories within that entity. According to Meissner (2018), the stratified status tracks designed by legal regulation of migration impacts configurations of "diversity" induced by migration at not only the national but also the local level. By creating these situations of legal and administrative classification at the border of and within the "migration state" (Hollifield 2006), migration feeds social engineering and population management techniques, promulgating "the technology of law" as a central governance tool. The global institutionalization and diffusion of the categories with the aim of defining, constituting, and organizing population diversity thus establish a form of "categorical infrastructure" of the modern nation-state (Brubaker 2015: 8). As rights and protections afforded by the state to different population categories become closely associated with social engineering, monitoring, and control, this categorical infrastructure inevitably translates into a system of civic stratification (Morris 2002) potentially feeding socioeconomic inequalities and other dimensions of social stratification.

Migration, Legal Categorization, and Inequality

Unequal access to resources

Legal migratory categorization feeds inequality through various mechanisms. The first and the most obvious of these concerns access to legal resources. Migratory categorizations are indeed immediately embedded in a stratified system of political, economic, and social rights: migrants with different legal status do not have the same rights to move across international borders or, sometimes, within them, the same rights to long-term settlement, the same rights to work, the same rights to receive welfare benefits, the same rights to vote, etc. Cross-disciplinary scholarship in sociology and legal studies shows how laws are omnipresent in immigrant lives and how they may take total control among the most vulnerable categories, such as undocumented migrants (Menjívar and Abrego 2012; Motomura 2014).

In addition to unequal rights, legal inequality expands into what can be called "administrative inequality."

This form of inequality is embedded in interactions with governmental bureaucracies, which are necessary to access status certifications in modern societies. Obtaining official documentation asserting status obliges migrants to dedicate a considerable amount of time and effort to red tape, paperwork, forms, fees, deadlines, etc. Loss of documents, translation issues, credential recognition, skills assessments, medical tests, language education, and, more recently, civic and cultural training are all examples of costly bureaucratic processes that often come with complex and ambiguous eligibility requirements and a labyrinthine mix of formalities and constraints that inevitably lead to situations of administrative stress (Jasso 2011). Administrative inequality might be the most blatant when it takes the form of inequality of treatment; lack of courtesy, long queues, and sometimes adversity and disrespect in public administrations are repeatedly observed and documented during interactions with migrants. These aspects of migration-related inequality culminate in abuses in detention centers, border patrol brutality in various forms, including forced separation of children from their parents, and killings (Carling 2007; Diaz and Kuhner 2009; Dreby 2012, 2015; Fix et al. 2018). Police and military enforcement of migratory categorization in particular can be a direct cause of death (Slack 2019). In the context of the increasing militarization of the borders, migration routes are becoming more dangerous than ever and security controls are shown to be more and more harmful (Eschbach et al. 1999; Carling 2007).[6]

The legal and administrative channel through which migration effects inequality may be paradoxically regarded as somehow operating "outside the rule of law." As highlighted by Motomura (2014), these regulations and practices are at odds with the democratic standards of human dignity, integrity, and individual protections. This means that migration opens up a certain amount of non-democratic space even within the most committed

democracies. In some countries, this space is institutionalized in immigration laws themselves; in most countries,
it is at least present in practice and through the discre-
tionary role of the state. In their treatment of migrants,
state-level institutions and agencies somehow benefit from
a sort of "dispensation" or opt-out from the standards
on equality of human rights with which they theoretically
comply. In this respect, undocumented migrants become
a form of pariah; they are constructed as unlawful and
as outside the law, which consequently often denies
them access to basic rights and subjects them to high
levels of abuse and disrespect, not to mention the risk
of detainment and deportation (Wong 2015). A prolific
scholarship at the cutting-edge of sociology, political
science, and legal studies highlights the ways in which
legal management of migration forges a system of legal
violence subjecting migrants to what Menjivar famously
refers to as "liminal legality" (see also Coutin 1998, 2000,
2011; De Genova 2002; Massey et al. 2002; Mize and
Swords 2010; Abrego 2011; Menjivar and Abrego 2012;
Kubal 2013).

In that sense, migration categorization opens the door
to one of the most powerful civic aspects of contemporary
inequality, one not only tolerated by most modern states
but actually designed, implemented, and organized by
their democratic institutions. There is some parallel to be
drawn here between migration and the criminal justice
system. Similar to crime and delinquency, migration
gives rise to legal categorization that is directly matched
to an uneven distribution of legal and civic resources.
Nonetheless, while the criminal justice system principally
relies on coercion and punishment as a central mechanism
of inequality, the migration-driven system of inequality
draws on opportunity hoarding and instruments of social
closure. It mainly consists of excluding migrants from
the advantages of citizenship (legal, social, political, and
economic, depending on configurations). The legal nature
of the categorizations that underlie these two systems

of inequality nonetheless lead to similar enforcement "techniques" including administrative, police, and military aspects. Yet moral and symbolic legitimizations of these systems are sharply different. The legitimization of the criminal justice system is grounded in the moral proscription of harming other individuals or groups and the functional threat provoked by crime and delinquency to order, peace, and social cohesion. The legitimization of the migratory legal system of inequality is principally tied to an exclusionist ideology of modern citizenship and its embeddedness in a mix of territorial, cultural, and ethnic criteria. Both systems are nonetheless intrinsically legally discriminatory; they map an uneven distribution of rights and obligations across inhabitants of the same countries, thus institutionalizing a legal sphere for discrimination within civic egalitarianism.

From the perspective of inequality theory, similar to the division of labor, the legal categorization of migrants provides a case of endogenous categorization, thus constituting a powerful example of the consubstantiality of categorization and distribution mechanisms. Nonetheless, while the division of labor is endogenously tied to the categorization of economic agents (between workers and capitalists or, more generally, between social classes), the legal channel through which migration affects inequality is authoritative and political in nature. It is closely related to what is often referred to as the performative dimension of the law (Bourdieu 1982). Figure 4.2 represents the specificity of the channel through which migration affects the elementary interaction between categorization and distribution in social stratification dynamics. The endogenous categorization driven by the legal management of migration puts into perspective the pivotal position usually conferred upon the division of labor as the mechanism of distribution of resources. Legal resources nested in legal and administrative categories of migration result in unequal life chances; in this sense, they are just as materialistic as jobs and money.

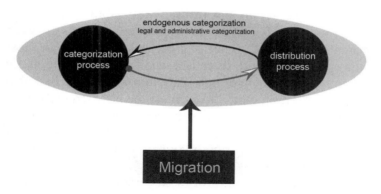

Figure 4.2 Migration and inequality: the legal channel

Nonetheless, and similar to other categorization processes, migratory categorizations also affect the distribution of other extra-legal types of resources. Once diffused in diverse social spheres and used in social interactions, legal categories of migration exert spillover effects, channeling migrants to opportunities or disadvantages that range from the very material to the moral and symbolic.

On the material side of the spectrum, legal categories of migration are implemented in labor market regulations, consequently determining access to jobs and positions.[7] The state's production of categories of migrants affects the ways they are constituted as a "laboring class" with the hierarchy of citizenship directly transported into the economic sector (Massey and Gelatt 2010). The most obvious example is the explicit regulation of labor markets along nationality lines, as access to public sector jobs is restricted to nationals in most countries. Beyond the national versus non-national dichotomy of workers, labor market segmentation along legal categories is also multidimensional, and it is explicitly based on nationality of origin in some social settings. In EU countries, for example, a tripartite distinction between national, EU member states,[8] and non-EU member states is legally implemented and determines access to positions in the labor markets. In other migratory contexts, socioeconomic rewards are even more explicitly tied to nationality; this is the case in most Gulf countries, where there is a legally enforced hierarchy not only between nationals and non-nationals, but also among the latter, with Westerners being extremely well paid in comparison to migrants from the global South. In these countries, "Western expats" seem to earn "wages of their nationality" or, some may say, of their "whiteness" (Le Renard 2019).

Like nationality, migratory categorizations determining legal status, types of permit, duration of stay, etc. also feed the segmentation of the labor force. Migration legal categorization indeed creates de facto socio-legal hierarchies of workers, making some of them more protected and some others more "exploitable," both fulfilling and reproducing the economic need for segmented labor markets (Massey et al. 2002). This explains the political economy type of tension that is fundamental to migration regulation policies, characterized by a necessary tradeoff between "openness" to admitting these migrant workers and the "bolting" and "hardening" that are necessary to restricting their rights and maintaining their status as formally unequal (Massey et al. 2002; Mize and Swords 2010; Hall and Greenman 2015).

Legal categorization is also shown to affect other dimensions of socioeconomic attainment in a variety of areas, such as health and well-being, geographical localization, housing, the criminal justice system, etc. Effects on health are shown to be mediated by health insurance coverage and medical expenditures (Carrasquillo et al. 2000; Castañeda et al. 2015; Martinez et al. 2015; Torres and Waldinger 2015). Legal status also has tangible psychological effects, impacting well-being and self-esteem (Menjivar 2006; Steel et al. 2011). These socioeconomic costs of the most vulnerable legal statuses might even affect second generations' outcomes in relation not only to health and well-being (Hainmueller et al. 2017) but also to educational attainment (Gonzales 2011; Greenman and Hall 2013). Finally, evidence shows that the criminal justice system treats citizens and non-citizens unequally. Light and colleagues (2014) highlight that the non-citizen penalty tends to have increased within racial categories during the last few decades in the United States. And, more generally, ethnographic research documents how legal status also affects lifestyles and social relations, feeding inequality mechanisms. Menjívar and Lakhani (2016) describe the long-term effects of legal processes on the lives of immigrants, their beliefs, practices and sense of the self, which they interpret in line with the Foucauldian notion of the "governmentality of the law," reflecting the disciplining power of the states on migrants' subjectivities. All things considered, in addition to rights and political status, legal categorization of migrants results in "real," sustainable and potentially transmissible economic inequalities (Aydemir 2011; Elrick and Lightman 2016).

On the symbolic side of the spectrum, legal categorization potentially translates into moral hierarchies and scales of "deservingness" (Alexander 1992; Fassin 2005). The national/alien elementary categorization is again a powerful example; there is indeed an underlying "natural status" in the concept of "national," most overtly expressed in the word "naturalization," which literally means "becoming natural" (Sayad 1993). The term encapsulates a whole range of moral and symbolic values that are associated with citizenship. The US law specifies, for example, that "good moral character" is required for foreign petitioners. This vague legal notion confers a considerable power on officers' assessment of an immigrant's "morals" during the application review (Aptekar 2015). This moral and symbolic dimension is in fact present in most legal categorizations. Numerous studies highlight the symbolic boundaries between legal and "illegal" migrants, emphasizing the role of anti-immigrant forces, the media and policymakers in the moral boundary work surrounding undocumented migration (Fassin et al. 1997; Fassin 2001; Capetillo-Ponce 2008; Chavez 2008; Yoo 2008; Massey and Riosmena 2010; Chauvin and Garcés-Mascareñas 2012; Barron et al. 2014). This "moral economy" of illegality plays an increasing role in anti-immigrant mobilizations in the United States, distinguishing between "good" and "bad" migrations and lauding the contribution of documented non-citizens while demonizing illegal migrants. Moral divisions between foreigners and nationals and among legal and non-legal migrations increasingly shape welfare politics (Newton 2008; Brown 2013). And even within legality, categories of migrants are increasingly becoming the locus of moral and symbolic negotiations. This is the case in the conflict over family reunion versus labor migrants in many European countries. Family reunion migrants, for instance, are constantly depicted as emblematic of the "undesired" nature of contemporary migration, which is mostly thought to be driven by supposedly non-legitimate "welfare magnets." The recent debate over "refugee" versus "migrant" in the context of the so-called "migrant crisis" also provides a powerful example of the moral and symbolic boundaries at work within the legal categorization of migrants (Zetter 2007; Crawley and Skleparis 2018; FitzGerald and Arar 2018). This boundary work is occurring at the state level but is also driven by UNHCR and a multitude of national and international organizations, privileging the rights and needs of refugees over migrants (Long 2013). This "categorical fetishism" (Crawley and Skleparis 2018) clearly reflects the ways in which legal categories of migration become cultural categories of worth and present scripts readily available to policymakers, the media, and the civil society. In this respect, the symbolic dimension of legal migratory categorization shares some commonalities with ethno-racial categorization (which is the focus of the next chapter). It nonetheless provokes different dynamics in the making and unmaking of inequality, creating divergent openings for rights claims. Indeed, and even if this symbolic dimension of legal categorization leaves some room for "political struggles" and "cultural negotiations" over "deservingness," it still relies heavily on documentation, paperwork, and administrative process, which is no longer the case for the ethnic and racial dimension, at least in most democratic countries. Chauvin and Garcés-Mascareñas (2014) describe the undocumented migrants' "fetishism of papers" as they scrupulously keep paper trails in the hope that this might help them prove deservingness in any future legalization (namely, in relation to work and tax paying). Migrants' attempts to fit into categories of inclusion constructed by the law might have some pernicious effects, reifying these categories and solidifying their deservingness boundaries. These dynamics, for instance, are described in the efforts deployed by migrants in order to comply with certain specific humanitarian categories (e.g., victim of violence, child or unaccompanied minor refugees) (Berger 2009; Lakhani 2013; Galli 2017).

All in all, legal categories of migration shape the individual lives of migrants. They have direct implications in terms of rights and status and also affect access to a wide range of material resources. They add to the multiple axes of differences in the immigration debate, complexifying worth and deservingness categories, and constitute "premier stratifying institutions" in modern societies (Stuart et al. 2015).

Legal de-/recategorization of immigrants and the remaking of inequality

One of the specificities of the legal categorization of migration lies in the fact that it is assigned formally, defined, and enforced by legitimate institutions. It thus falls into the imposition type of categorization (Tilly 2003, 2005), involving more top-down techniques than participation and negotiations. Therefore, the degree to which the legal categories of migration result in dynamics of group self-identification – or groupness (Brubaker 2002) – is relatively weak. In this sense, migratory categorization is fundamentally nominalistic; refugees, guest workers, temporary workers, and even undocumented migrants are "labels" that externally define groups (Zolberg et al. 1986; Donato and Armenta 2011; Lochak 2013). They sharply differ in this respect from categories of identity – at least, they did not emerge as such. Their social construction process is straightforwardly traceable. This presents a convenience for researchers on these questions: it is indeed possible to identify specific "events" (laws, decrees, implementation of migration policies, police or legal procedures, etc.) that map the dynamics of migration legal categorization (Calavita 1992; Phillips and Massey 1999).

From a policy point of view, the nominalist character of migratory categorization provides avenues for egalitarian action through legal de- and/or recategorization. This is initially observable at the individual level; since migratory categorization is firmly connected to access to resources, as discussed above, immigrant social mobility becomes closely tied to "administrative mobility," or mobility across legal categories. The most impressive mobility is, of course, the one that governs the passage from foreigner to national. Recent scholarship has been documenting significant effects of naturalization on the reduction of inequality between natives and immigrants, particularly in the labor market (Bratsberg et al. 2002; Fougère and Safi 2009; Corluy et al. 2011; Steinhardt 2012; Gathmann and Keller 2014; Hainmueller et al. 2015). Some of these effects are simply related to the fact that citizenship acquisition opens the way to the public sector, which constitutes a considerable share of the labor market in most economies. Some others are related to lower discrimination facing nationals in comparison to foreigners. Here, the context of EU enlargement offers an interesting case-study. Ruhs (2017) investigated the effect of acquiring EU status on the relative earnings of Central and Eastern European migrants who had been working in the UK before the 2004 enlargement. He found that EU status had a statistically significant and positive impact that is mainly channeled through easily changing jobs and career mobility. All in all, this "naturalization premium" explains the inevitable instrumental dimension of access to citizenship that may, although still marginally, lead to the selling and buying of passports as a form of redistributive process (Joppke 2019).

Although empirical work is scarcer due to a lack of data and the difficulty of disentangling strictly causal effects, de-categorization of unauthorized migration through legalization is shown to lead to similar egalitarian dynamics (Hall et al. 2010). And beyond these most powerful categorical mobilities, obtaining work permits, moving from temporary to permanent residency, and other changes in legal status probably have similar positive effects on access to resources (Lowell and Avato 2014).

The degree to which migratory de- and recategorization induce egalitarian dynamics is an empirical issue: it varies along national and local differences in the ways citizenship and legal status are tied to labor market regulations. Some studies also suggest that these egalitarian effects are heterogeneous across individual class, education, gender, or ethnoracial attributes. The naturalization "premium" is thus shown to be more significant for non-European migrants in many OECD countries (OECD 2010). Categorical legal mobility seems, on the contrary, to be of little benefit for some disadvantaged categories of migrant workers, as shown by the example of female caregiver migrants in Canada whose structural position in the labor market, as well as the emotional and symbolic aspects of their job, are so determinant that changes in legal status do not make such a difference (Banerjee et al. 2018).

While the research described above provides individual examples of de-/recategorization, collective dynamics such as regularization campaigns, changes in naturalization policies, immigration law reforms, etc. may present massive impacts. This advocates for thorough interdisciplinary studies of specific programs. Some scholars argue that certain less visible forms of collective recategorization have been progressively achieved within international law, through the (ongoing) building of global human rights legislation. The expansion of a legal apparatus that transcends national borders (through the UN, the European Union, the International Court of Justice, etc.) plays an important role in compelling nation-states to extend membership to their immigrant population, alleviating inequalities, at least in terms of rights and political status, provoked by migration (Bauböck 1994; Soysal 1994). Historians draw attention to the fact that this "emancipatory potential" of universal citizenship norms can be found in the use of "its language" in many decisive egalitarian struggles; from the abolition of slavery to contemporary civil rights movements, including feminist and worker struggles.

On the whole, the legal channel that connects migration to inequality dynamics provides a powerful example of the effectiveness of "jumping categorical inequality" in the dismantling of inequality (Korzeniewicz and Moran 2009: 107). Legally generated categories can be linked to specific procedures – administrative at the individual level, political at the collective level – making the crossing between categories possible. In that sense, migration itself represents a powerful "administrative mobility." In addition to geographic mobility, migration opens the door to transgressing powerful citizenship categories that are constitutive of worldwide inequality. Migrants also engage in the processes of crossing "boundaries" of citizenship while crossing state borders. Conversely, strict border control, by reinforcing the assignment of citizenship to place of birth, helps perpetuate the global system of citizenship inequality (Pritchett 2006).

Egalitarian dynamics are nonetheless not only related to individual categorical-crossing or collective and institutional reforms that change the categories themselves. The categories may remain stable, but "cultural shifts" and symbolic renegotiations over their meaning may ultimately lead to their inegalitarian nature being alleviated. Even if legal categorization of migrants stems largely from state-level top-down procedures, ethnographic research subtly shows how the intrinsic ambiguity of legal categorization, and the "twilight statuses" it creates (Motomura 2008: 2048), leave some room for agency, claims-making, and negotiations. In her thorough study of Salvadoran immigrants' claims for political asylum in the United States, Coutin (2000) highlights the inherent mismatch between legal categories and their meanings within immigrant lives, thus enhancing a form of "legal consciousness." Studies in the same vein show how refugees and undocumented migrants recognize the empowering power of the law despite their being subject to institutional "legal violence" (Menjívar 2006; Abrego 2011). Struggles and renegotiations over immigration laws are conducted by both migrants and natives; and Voss and Bloemraad (2011) analyze the social determinants, schemes, and narratives underlying this "rallying for immigrant rights" through the case study of one of the larger protests over immigrant rights in the world: the 2006 mobilization in the United States against the Border Protection, Antiterrorism and Illegal Immigration Control Act. In France, the basilica of Saint-Denis became a symbolic place, frequently at the center of pro-migrant demonstration and mobilizations for regularization (Barron et al. 2011). Recent pro-migrant demonstrations in European countries (in Germany and Spain in particular) urging governments to host more refugees show that grounds for such mobilization still exist, despite overall less favorable attitudes toward immigration.

Recent studies also emphasize the role of immigrant offspring when it comes to their rights. Since most legal statuses are not transmissible across generations, there is some avenue for a generational dismantling of legal categorizations in most immigrant societies (Nicholls 2013; Street et al. 2017). One may note here a more general feature of inequality driven by the law: it creates status inequality that potentially becomes contested in the name of the law itself. In these ways, immigrant protests have been participating in the legal reshaping of citizenship boundaries in many immigrant societies (Tyler and Marciniak 2013).

These symbolic struggles over legal categorization strongly interact with other symbolic classifications, namely those related to race and ethnicity. Many legal scholars have highlighted the ways in which immigrant laws rely on ethnoracial hierarchies with the pernicious result of reifying and stabilizing them (Calavita 2005, 2007; Motomura 2007, 2014). Legal categories may also be used by immigrants themselves in a strategy of distancing themselves from stigmatized ethnic minorities to avoid disadvantaged positions in the ethnoracial hierarchy; in this context, the refugee status may become an asset (Brown 2011). Legal categorization of migration interacts with ethnoracial categorization, creating space for "liminal status" (Motomura 2008). In this way, these categorizations contribute to the construction of racialized hierarchies of membership.

On the whole, the effect of migration on political inequality sheds light on the dark sides of contemporary forms of political membership of nation-states. The seminal work of Marshall (1950; 1964) considered that, with equalizing rights, modern citizenship lays the foundation for a virtuous cycle enhancing political and social rights; in other words, politically empowering citizenship leads, in the Marshallian world, to socioeconomic equality. Marshall's obvious bias has been to exclusively focus on the internal dimension of citizenship. Migration patterns clearly show that the external dimension of citizenship is one of the most powerful inequality producers worldwide. As demonstrated in this chapter, migration is particularly valuable to social stratification theory because it provides an example of endogenous categorization that puts the distinctiveness of the division of labor in producing inequality into question. The unequal distribution of legal resources is directly related to administrative processes of migrant categorization resulting in unequal *life chances*; they are, in that sense, just as materialistic as labor, money, and power. One may nonetheless debate the autonomy of legal categorization in the production of inequality in situations of migration. Although these categories are originally nominally constructed, scholars highlight their overlap with identity-type categories (ethnicity, race, and nationhood), which leads them to potentially participate in group boundary-making dynamics, the focus of the next chapter.

— 5 —

The Ethnoracial Channel: Migration, Group Boundary-Making, and Ethnoracial Classifications

This chapter sketches some analytics of the link between migration and the ethnic/racial dimension of inequality. In parallel with its relation to endogenous distribution/categorization processes described in Chapters 3 and 4, migration interferes with exogenous categorization processes that consist in allocating individuals to ethnoracial categories. While migration's connections to ethnic and racial studies immediately appear as natural, their foundations remain relatively undertheorized in the social sciences literature. In contrast with direct associations of migration to supposedly increasing ethnic diversity/fragmentation within nation-states, approaches that reflect on the ways in which migrants *fit in* a given ethnoracial order have recently gained ground. They describe the ways in which migration gives rise to situations of ethnoracial reclassification. This chapter reviews recent developments in this rich literature, in an attempt to disentangle mechanisms through which migration interferes with categorization processes, affecting the formation of ethnoracial groups and the ways in which these group boundary reconfigurations affect social inequality. Throughout the following discussion, I choose to combine the concepts of ethnicity and race in the use of the expression "ethnoracial." I will begin, therefore, by clarifying this choice of terminology.

The Ethnoracial Dimension of Inequality

From ethnicity and race to ethnoracial formation

Ethnicity and race are closely related concepts that often appear hand in hand in scholarship (along with other neighboring concepts such as nation or culture). There nonetheless remain nuances in their meanings and connotations, and there is some difference in their usage depending on national contexts or the specific group marker to which they refer. As scholars still differ on whether it is more theoretically accurate to consider race or ethnicity as an umbrella concept,[1] their conjunction in one expression – *ethnoracial* – may appear to be a "soft compromise." Nonetheless, I argue that their combined use in relation to social inequality is theoretically grounded.[2]

First, and most obviously, race and ethnicity both refer to human classifications into groups. The distinctions upon which these classifications build vary historically in relation to structural and cultural contexts (Banton 1998). The shared meaning of race/ethnicity is consequently perpetually subject to transformations and negotiations. Based on these ideas, a constructivist consensus emerged in the second half of the twentieth century, instilling the diverse social science literature involved in ethnic and racial studies (Brubaker 2009; Saperstein et al. 2013; Wimmer 2013). This constructivist turn opened the way to effervescent pluridisciplinary research documenting the ways in which group classifications form and evolve. Social psychologists have been inquiring into the cognitive mechanisms involved in categorization grounded in social differences, investigating their relation to behavioral biases (Brubaker et al. 2004). One of social psychology's most decisive contributions to the field lies in its emphasis on the role of "social cognition" and the way it builds on categorical associations, mental shortcuts, and stereotyping. This scholarship also stresses the impact of the social dimension of individual identity (or what is referred to as social identity) and its relation to group favoritism and status biases (Deaux 1993; Fiske et al. 2002; Hogg and Ridgeway 2003; Harris and Fiske 2006). The processes that connect these micro foundations of ethnoracial categorizations to their macro social ubiquity are understood to be of a cultural nature (DiMaggio 1997; Lamont et al. 2014). Research at the intersection of semiotic and cultural sociology refers to "meaning-making" processes to describe the ways in which the social significance conferred upon belonging to a group is constructed, becomes increasingly shared in social settings, and is often subject to continuous contestation and negotiation within different types of social interactions. Scholars in sociology and political sciences are particularly concerned with the ways in which these classifications acquire a symbolic and moral dimension, shaping the hierarchy of social relations and affecting the individual and collective sense of belonging in a way that fosters political contestation and future reclassification. In a variation on Omi and Winant's (1994) influential contribution (see also Saperstein et al. 2013), I will refer to these diverse and multileveled social processes of meaning-making surrounding group distinctions using the expression "ethnoracial formation."

In search of an impossible taxonomy

Even though the social meanings of ethnicity and race are differently charged, and despite their distinct historical uses and connotations (Banton 2018), the contemporary social science literature tends to understand both of them in relation to meaning-making processes grounded in social differences. The relevance of their combination into one expression stems from the difficulty of drawing a straightforward separating line between the two concepts based on a taxonomy of the social differences to which they refer (i.e., ethnic/racial markers). It is nonetheless relatively common to use the term "race" in reference to biological or phenotypic criteria. Racial markers are commonly understood to be visible, durable, inalterable, and transmissible; skin tone is one of the markers that most frequently conform to this type of understanding of race. Conversely, typical perceptions of ethnicity draw associations with more malleable markers; often considered "cultural," these markers more frequently respond to social contexts and may be subject to instrumental change that renders them more or less salient depending on the setting (Bonilla-Silva 1999; Smith 2014). One may mention language, religion, norms, values, and lifestyles among the most emblematic ethnic markers. Anthropological and historical research has nonetheless questioned this marker-driven contrast between race and ethnicity. Some social configurations have certain similarities with "racial relations" despite the "culturalness" of the marker in which the group boundary is embedded. For instance, religious affiliations may be invested in the shaping of rigid relations of conflict and domination between groups. In such contexts, and beyond the system of beliefs, norms, and practices that they entail, religious affiliations sometimes become "incorporated markers." A biological connotation is also perceptible in ethnic belonging that draws on a common history, language, norms, and traditions: the frequent encapsulation of group membership in the "blood-tie" metaphor is emblematic in this respect. The racialization of people of Jewish or Moorish background in sixteenth-century Spain, the oppression and extermination of European Jews during World War II, and the current situation of Muslims in Europe all provide powerful examples of the limits of analytical separation between the racial and the ethnic (Bunzl 2005; Modood

2005; Gotanda 2011; Foner 2015). Typical racial markers may, on the other hand, acquire an "ethnic flavor" as soon as individuals identify with them. One may refer in that sense to the ethnicization of the African American group during the civil rights struggle in the United States (Omi and Winant 1994; Cornell and Hartmann 2004). The "Negritude" movement that emerged in the colonial and postcolonial contexts, and which has been quite influential in some Caribbean societies, is also emblematic of this sort of ethnic/cultural approach to skin color – commonly regarded as a typical racial marker (Césaire 1987; Hall 1994). In short, to quote Wimmer, "one and the same group might be treated as a race at one point in history and as another type of ethnic category at another" (2013: 8). These translations from ethnicity to race and vice versa hint at the need to move away from the dialectic nature/culture underlying the distinctions between the two concepts. Ethnoracial categorization processes are characterized by "primordialist claims" that make them fundamentally "essentializing" categorizations (Cornell and Hartmann 1998). The markers that rule, in certain contexts, the allocation of individuals to ethno-racial groups (language, skin color, religion, nationality, origin, etc.) share a relatively high responsiveness to essentialization processes and consequently tend to be perceived as ascriptive.

It must be stressed here that this does not necessarily preclude the fact that the "essence" of the marker invested in group boundary dynamics affects, at least partly, the social relations between the groups defined across these boundaries. Indeed, Brubaker (2009) argues that, while expanding the field by integrating the study of race, ethnicity, and nationality is analytically useful, it is also instructive to think about the distinctiveness of the inequality mechanisms associated with each type of marker.[3] This is exactly what he aims at in his *Ground for Difference* (2015), in which he compares categorization embedded in culture, language, skin color, citizenship, etc.

This position can be understood as advocating a "soft" social constructivism, which, even while acknowledging the contingent feature of group boundary construction, remains attentive to the specificity of the associations of cognitive, semiotic, and cultural processes with the particular human attributes invested in ethnoracial categorization. Social psychologists highlight, for example, that markers inscribed on the human body present some specificities in terms of social cognition that probably affect the type of social relations they help to shape. Rapidly visible and readily available for mental allocation to categories, they entail a certain "cognitive efficiency" upon encounter, which straightforwardly stimulates the activation of a whole range of conscious and unconscious biases (Ridgeway and Balkwell 1997; Wilkins et al. 2010).

In addition, it should be noted that, even if, following some influential scholars in the field, one commits to a definition of race that stresses its inscription on the body, there remains a high level of uncertainty in associating racial groups' boundaries with objectivized body markers. Winant (2000) argues that it is precisely this uncertainty that might at least partially explain the discomfort one feels with respect to the notion of race, a malaise that can be translated into rejection of the use of the word altogether. Even when one agrees on the potency of skin color in creating meaningful group categories in a wide diversity of contemporary societies, the ways in which the marker translates into racial categories lends itself poorly to direct empirical objectivation.[4] Research in the field is consequently confronted with a kind of empirical elusiveness.

The discomfort with the concept, moreover, is rooted in the fact that a historically specific conception of race – which attributes a hierarchical moral worth to human phenotypes – is still relatively dominant in the social and political imagination, leading to a sort of all-out demonization of the term. According to Banton (1998), this conception corresponds to an understanding of race as "types" of people; it is relatively recent (nineteenth century) and is related to the specific context in which social Darwinism emerged in the West. The predominance of this particular conception of race has resulted in a sort of decontextualization of the concept, in contradiction to its being understood as the product of perpetual processes of cultural negotiation. The conjunction of race and ethnicity in research that focuses on their consequences in terms of inequality helps overcome this restrictive understanding of race, grounded in the social Darwinist legacy.

The adoption of a unifying ethnoracial lens is all the more relevant when the focus is on the effects of migration on societies. Population movements trigger the circulation of a variety of markers – virtually all those that may be associated with human classification (body-related markers, language, religion, family structures, norms, lifestyles, etc.). Additionally, migration has the specificity of disseminating nationality-based markers, which argues in favor of Brubaker's integrated approach of ethnicity, race, and nation.[5] In the last section of this chapter, I will deal with the effect of migration on national boundary dynamics, understood as the identity dimension of citizenship that also represents a particular form of ethnoracial categorization.[6]

The elementary processes of ethnoracial formation

Literature that focuses on ethnoracial boundary-work has been flourishing over the decades (Barth 1969; Lamont and Molnar 2002; Wimmer 2008). It draws attention to the central role of identification in the allocation of individuals to groups (Brubaker and Cooper 2000). Identification may proceed by self-definition (internal, subjective) or/and third-part definition (external, assigned; Jenkins, 1994). Assigned identification consists in delimiting out-groups through imposed, and most often authoritative, classifications. In a pioneering article, Lyman and Douglass (1973) use a strikingly expressive formulation – "alter-casting" – to designate this process. This expression stresses the fact that the delimitation of the boundary is drawn from outside the group: as a result, assignment processes are particularly effective in producing categories that are related to visible-on-the-body markers (e.g., traditional clothing, visible religious symbols, skin tone, hair type, somatic features, etc.). Self-identification, conversely, is grounded in a belief in within-group "similarities" in which a sense of group belonging is invested. Weber's (1921: 130) conceptualization of ethnicity as "subjective belief in a community of origin" remains a key reference in the definition of self-identification processes.

These definitions may lead to more pronounced associations between assignment and racial categorization, on the one hand, and self-identification and ethnic categorization, on the other. Yet, the distinction remains ideal-typical to the extent that – and herein lies an additional justification for combining ethnicity and race – assignment and self-identification are nested and mutually affecting processes. The relational nature of these elementary categorization processes – the fact that they emanate from encounters and interactions between human beings – leads to their consubstantiality. Research on whiteness in the North American context emphasizes that the assignment of African-originated populations, forcibly displaced as slaves and originally characterized by a wide human diversity (cultural, linguistic, religious, and even phenotypic, etc.), to the "black" racial group corollary entails the construction of the "non-black" group as white and the self-identification of European descendants, as varied as they were at the time, to this unified group identity (Frankenberg 1993; McDermott and Samson 2005; Ward 2008).

Moreover, the connection between categorization and distribution processes in the production and reproduction of social stratification dynamics (see Chapter 2, Figure 2.1) makes the outcome of the back-and-forth processes of self-identification and assignment highly dependent on the real "context" of power relations between the groups involved in ethnoracial formation dynamics. Here, the sociological perspective underlies the struggle over the symbolic dimension of social stratification, a "struggle over categorization" or "classification struggle" (Bourdieu 1984). Jenkins formulates this interrelation between ethnoracial categorization and power relation very clearly, defining ethnoracial formation processes as dependent on "the capacity of one group to successfully impose its categories of ascription upon another set of people, and to the resources which the categorized collectivity can draw upon to resist, if need be, that imposition" (1997: 23). This tension between self- and alter-categorization is perceptible in the imperfect overlapping measured in studies that ask people to categorize others based on photos, or in the ones that compare self-identification to alter-identification (Feliciano 2016; Roth 2016).

From Ethnoracial Boundaries to Ethnoracial Inequality

From a heuristic point of view, it is useful to situate ethnoracial categorization outside the mechanisms of resource distribution. As discussed in Chapter 2, in systems of social stratification, exogenous categorical differences that become widely used in a social setting translate into status distinctions that are capable of creating independent dynamics of social inequality (Ridgeway 2014). Unlike legal categorization, implications of ethnoracial differences are not necessarily formal; they are triggered intersubjectively as a sort of externality in human interactions. And unlike the division of labor, these categorizations do not directly result from a biased distribution of material resources. There are nonetheless some historical situations that witness a high degree of overlapping between these three mechanisms of inequality (economic, legal, ethnoracial). The US Jim Crow era and South Africa's apartheid system demonstrate powerful intersection between state-imposed and ethnoracial categorizations (Mangum 1940).

Ethnoracial categorization may also be quite "efficiently" matched to the division of labor, as is the case in slave-based economies.[7] These examples have been used in reductionist stances, undermining the ethnoracial dimension and presenting it as a sort of veil that hides the real, hard mechanisms of inequality embedded in the economy or the polity. The recent convergence of structural and cultural streams in stratification scholarship puts this reductionism into perspective, assessing the autonomy of categorical mechanisms of inequality and their crucial role in the reproduction and durability of stratification systems, including those that guarantee high levels of legal egalitarianism to their members. The concept of status, defined as the moral and symbolic value attributed to a social category, is crucial in bridging the gap between cultural and structural approaches. Similar to gender, social differences involved in ethnoracial formation have status implications; they form status-based social differences and lead to various types of status biases in social interactions (Ridgeway 2013). Status expectations function as a form of common knowledge, one shared on both sides of the ethnoracial boundary, biasing attitudes and representations, albeit unconsciously and unintentionally for the most part. Thus, they reinforce inequality in a self-generating way (Greenwald and Banaji 1995; Devine 2001; Bertrand et al. 2005; Greenwald and Krieger 2006; Quillian 2008). By integrating the individual subjective interpretation of the social structure to the analysis of social stratification, these perspectives connect the micro and macro dimensions of inequality.

This iterative characteristic of ethnoracial formation, referred to as a "field" in Bourdieusian terms, points to the embeddedness of the ethnoracial mechanisms of inequality in the social structure. Winant considers that there is here a "key element in racial formation," which consists of "the link between meaning and structure, between what race means in a particular discursive practice and how, based upon such interpretations, social structures are racially organized" (2004: p. 200). I will refer to this ethnoracial dimension of social stratification that consists in socially positioned ethnoracial categories as the "ethnoracial order." The concept of order here captures the fact that ethnoracial meaning-making gains grounds in relation to the groups' social positions (Kim 1999; Hochschild et al. 2012; Emirbayer and Desmond 2015). The ethnoracial order thus refers to the mapping of existing ethnoracial categorizations onto the spheres of resource distribution. History testifies to many dark areas of the use of ethnoracial categorization as an underlying structure for systematic violence, coercion, and even extermination. Even within contemporary liberal and egalitarianist modern states, there is a colossal amount of scientific evidence that documents ample and enduring biases in the distribution of resources between ethnoracial groups in a variety of spheres such as the labor market, housing, education, health, well-being, etc. Hiring discrimination, for example, whether statistical or taste-based, assessed in many studies in the United States and Europe, emanates from biased distributional mechanisms that operate on the basis of underlying ethnoracial categorizations (Pager and Shepherd 2008). In the United States, despite policy changes, there is no evidence of decline in racial hiring discrimination over recent decades (Quillian et al. 2017). Existing ethnoracial categories similarly feed potential biases in the distribution of legal resources; in many societies, immigration laws have frequently used ethnoracial categories as a platform for the implementation of policies that range from border control to the allocation of economic, political, and social rights and the acquisition of citizenship (Bashi 2004; Calavita 2005; FitzGerald 2017).

US history provides powerful examples of racialized migration laws, not only in regulating entry (e.g., the prohibition of Chinese immigration with the passing of the 1882 Chinese Exclusion Act, which was broadened to include most Asian migrants by 1917) and naturalization (e.g., the historic limitation of naturalization to whites), but also in "denaturalization" (Calavita 2007; Cook-Martín and FitzGerald 2010). It was only in 1952, with the Immigration and Nationality Act, that discrimination in naturalization was officially prohibited.

While overt racialization of citizenship has become rarer in postwar democratic countries in general, research shows that immigration laws and policies are still deeply racialized in many countries. In contradiction to official claims of colorblindness, the French state worked up a whole range of racialized citizenship categories in colonial Algeria and also in metropolitan France shortly after decolonization, principally with the aim of distinguishing between "colonial French" and "Algerian Muslims" and later between French "return colonials" and "Algerian Muslim immigrants" (Alba and Silberman 2002; Couto 2013; Escafré-Dublet et al. 2018). More recently, in 2005, France introduced the use of DNA tests as an instrument of family reunion validation, with the aim of obstructing the entry of supposedly extended family relations from African sending societies. In many European countries, the management of the recent refugee crisis used regulations and administrative practices that relied heavily on an intersection of nationality-based and ethnoracial categorizations of asylum seekers; the case of Christian Syrians is quite revealing in this regard.

While these examples illustrate the ways in which ethnoracial categorizations are imported into the spheres of resource distribution, thus sustaining social inequality and contributing to its reproduction, it is useful to think about the dynamics of ethnoracial formation processes as "outcome-uncertain" or "open-ended." If ethnoracial categories form an order, ongoing ethnoracial formation processes may transform or alter existing categorizations, destabilizing the ethnoracial order. In other terms, ethnoracial de-categorization and recategorization may also alleviate inequality; categorical shifts potentially have a "redistributive" impact. This was undeniably the case with the civil rights movement in the United States, which can be understood as the materialization of symbolic ethnoracial reconfigurations into egalitarian outcomes in the legal and socioeconomic spheres. More generally, negotiations over patterns of ethnoracial categorizations in the context of affirmative action or diversity-promoting policies are among the most powerful illustrations of the egalitarian drift of ethnoracial recategorization (Martiniello and Simon 2005; Simon 2008). The use of official "ethnoracial statistics" to monitor anti-discrimination policies in democratic contexts such as the United States, Canada, the United Kingdom, and New Zealand not only redistributes material resources such as jobs and housing. Symbolic resources are also at stake, since these statistics most often involve a form of requalification of historically oppressed or discredited groups. This at least partly explains why these categories are the subject of political mobilization that can be regarded as "struggles for recognition." Although one should recall that state-level implementation of such categorization is historically correlated with ethnoracial violence, massive and undeniable evidence of ethnoracial inequality exerts growing pressure on Western egalitarian countries to use such categorizations in the conception and implementation of equal opportunity policies (Simon 2012; Simon et al. 2015). Whether this pressure ultimately leads to the incorporation of ethnoracial categorization into equal opportunity policies depends on the legal and political context and the effectiveness of minority collective mobilization. From this point of view, the use of ethnoracial categorization in policy reflects the power relations between groups in a society, not just its ethnic and racial composition (Hirschman et al. 2000). In Europe, due to a general reluctance to use any direct measurement of ethnoracial categorization, the emergence of these policies relies heavily on a migratory-based categorization (Simon 2017). Migratory background is therefore understood as a proxy for minority status. In the next section, I discuss the limitations of such a notion.

All in all, ethnorcial classifications, understood as historicized social classifications based on human distinctions, affect stratification dynamics. Similar underlying mechanisms that result in ethnoracial inequality may nonetheless contribute to dismantling it; while the idea of an "order" emphasizes the hierarchical dimensions of ethnoracial categorization, it also suggests that this type of inequality is responsive to change, negotiations, and reconfigurations. In the next section, I will focus on investigating the effect of migration on these reconfigurations.

Migration, Ethnoracial Recategorization, and the Reconfiguration of Inequality

The developments referred to above for the sake of clarifying the processes involved in ethnoracial formation constitute the foundations of the more specific discussion that I move to in the next pages, focusing on the ways in which migration affects ethnoracial formation and thereby inequality dynamics. But first it must be stressed that, contrary to the widely believed association between migration and ethnoracial diversity – often with supposed implications in terms of social cohesion and trust – migration is not systematically conducive to "ethnoracial diversity." The relation between migration and ethnicity/race is actually ambivalent. It is useful to recall, for instance, that immigration and race have traditionally been presented as "nearly polar opposites" in the American experience (Bean and Bell-Rose 1999: 3). Immigrants were often depicted as being antagonistic toward the African American, minority; their "optimism," "hard work," and "success" were frequently opposed to the African Americans; lack of full incorporation. Undoubtedly with the aim of opposing the biological racism that was dominant at the time, the first approaches to immigration in US sociology, namely in the pioneering work of the Chicago School, built on the immigrant assimilation process as an analogy (Blauner 1972) that predicts the attenuation and the virtual absorption of racial minorities (including African Americans) – which is strictly opposite to the depiction of immigration's effect in terms of ethnoracial diversification.

Nonetheless, and to quote from Bean and Bell-Rose again, "although it is misleading to treat the dynamics of immigration and race as essentially similar, neither is it satisfactory to treat race and immigration as completely separate phenomena" (1999: 5). While one may reasonably point out that the production of racial distinction in the United States is tied to the "involuntary migration" of African slaves, ethnoracial classifications are not always produced in the context of population movements; such relations may develop between "indigenous" groups (Richmond 1978). And more fundamentally, rather than diversification, migration can lead to ethnoracial homogenization; this is the case, for example, with ethnic affinity-driven migrations among which those that provide access to "ethnic citizenship" are the most emblematic (for example, *ethnic German* migrants to Germany, *ethnic Hungarian* migrants in Hungary, *ethnic Russian* migrants in Russia, and *Jewish* migrants to Israel). In these cases, migration counterintuitively produces "ethnic unmixing" (Brubaker 1998).

Rather than considering migration as an intrinsic factor of (ethnoracial) diversity,[8] theory-building should focus on the ways in which it potentially affects and reconfigures ongoing ethnoracial categorizations (Richmond 1956; Lee and Bean 2004; Foner et al. 2018). To illustrate this argument, it is helpful to use a simple hypothetical example. Let's take a context of strict physical group separation based on rigid material conditions (there is no way group A members encounter, communicate with, or even access information on group B members). If (a few) group A members happen to have managed to cross these previously impassable borders (thus becoming migrants in group B), their migration gives rise to "new situations" of social encounters, where existing social categorization used in interactions may prove to be fallible. By introducing people who have not been previously categorized within readily available categorization systems in particular social settings, migration potentially gives rise to new situations of classification (Tilly 2003). It must be stressed that the "novelty" of these situations of classification does not necessarily derive from the "types" of people that migration brings to a social setting, or the essence of their "difference." New situations of classification may also arise when migrants retain markers that are already salient and meaningful in the destination society, as I will develop below in the cases of black Mexican or West Indian migrants in the United States. In addition to the virtual novelty of human difference markers in themselves, migration potentially introduces variations in the interpretations of these markers, opening the way to a series of cultural negotiations and symbolic classifications. In this sense, ethnoracial reclassifications in situations of migration powerfully illustrate the contingency of ethnoracial meanings.

The simplified idea of abrupt encounter with no prior contact is, of course, excessively schematic; new situations of reclassification often take place in contexts where prior encounters did occur, or where at least some information has already circulated across individuals and groups involved in these encounters, carrying meanings and symbolic materials that potentially affect the dynamics of recategorization. In other words, migration-induced ethnoracial boundary reconfigurations build heavily on existing ethnoracial classifications; they are fundamentally historicized, path-dependent processes. This simplified framework nonetheless helps us understand the uniqueness of the ethnoracial formation moment provoked by the European transatlantic migration at the turn of the sixteenth century, as pointed out by many historians. Enhanced by technological innovation – progress in the scope and reach of naval transportation

– this unique migratory experience quite abruptly put together individuals and groups that were "total strangers" in the sense that no prior encounters or information could be used as building blocks for this new encounter. This unique ethnoracial formation moment consequently led to fundamental "classification doubts," which engendered questions about the political, religious, and even human status of the "indigenous" populations (the Valladolid debate of 1550–1).[9] Scholars who emphasize this line of interpretation of the European Conquista tend to intrinsically relate race to this specific historical moment; the modern concept of race is, in this sense, a "European invention" (Hanke 1970; Goldberg 1993; Fredrickson 2002). In the current era of intense globalization, at least in terms of communication and circulation of information, contemporary human migration is certainly quite distant from this specific historical moment; nonetheless, it entails similar elementary mechanisms related to new encounters and human intersubjective and collective reclassifications that potentially destabilize social stratification systems, mapping new categories of inequalities.

Figure 5.1 represents the ethnoracial channel through which migration affects inequality. This channel is determined by dynamics of ethnoracial formation in situations of migration induced by the interplay between assignment and self-identification as proximate mechanisms. Migration's effect on ethnoracial formation potentially alters the distribution of resources; however, contrary to the first two channels, the relation here is exogenous and more open-ended in nature. As discussed in detail hereafter, this translates to a wide variability of cases in outcomes concerned by this channel. I more specifically distinguish between dynamics that affect the host societies' ethnoracial order and those that take place at the transnational and global levels. On each of these two dimensions, I will discuss dynamics that consolidate the ethnoracial order before elaborating on those that destabilize it. Table 5.1 provides a summary of this discussion.

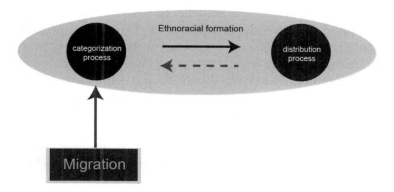

Figure 5.1 Migration and inequality: the ethnoracial channel

Table 5.1 Migration and ethnoracial boundary dynamics at the national and global levels

	Within-nation ethnoracial formation	Global ethnoracial formation
Solidification	Fitting in, fitting up, fitting down, boundary shifting, boundary crossing	Nation-building Nationalistic backlash, (re)defining the national as anti-migrant
Destabilization	Introducing new categories "Complex ethnicity" Weakening the association between ethnoracial categories and the allocation of resources	Transnational transfer of categorizations Reconfiguration of ethnoracial categories investing transnational markers

Migration and within-nation ethnoracial reconfigurations

Migrants enter destination societies characterized by existing ethnoracial classification systems that are more or less tied to the distribution of resources. Their arrival brings about the question of their categorization within this system, opening up "ethnoracial formation moments" in which the assignment and self-identification components interrelate, creating a variety of possible configurations. Assignment of some migrant groups to stigmatized symbolic categories is well documented in the literature. Research shows that it often consists of pointing out their supposed moral imperfections, their "laziness" and its correlated reliance on the welfare state, their unbridled sexuality and its effect on their fertility, and their violence sometimes in relation to presumably archaic cultures, social norms or religions, etc. These migrant traits, which are recurrent in anti-immigration and xenophobic narratives across many societies, are often portrayed in an essentializing fashion, sometimes taking explicit biological forms (Lee and Fiske 2012). Some scholars refer to this essentialization as denoting a process of "racialization of immigration" (Silverstein 2005). If these mostly assigned immigrant traits are powerful mainly because of the fundamental (legal and economic) vulnerability of migrants within host societies (as discussed in Chapters 3 and 4), the intersubjective characteristic of ethnoracial formation leaves considerable space for negotiations, in which migrants' agency proves to be crucial. They mobilize, whether individually or/and collectively, a wide range of socioeconomic, cultural, legal, and sometimes phenotypical resources while working out the ways in which they "fit in" existing classifications. The combination of these assignments and self-identification processes leads to a considerable amount of variation in the final outcomes of ethnoracial formation in situations of migration, across individuals and groups, either in local social settings or in the wider national context.

For the sake of analytical concision, below I disentangle two broad directions of these dynamics: fitting the ethnoracial order and transforming the ethnoracial order. The first direction most often leads to the solidification of the ethnoracial dimension of social inequality within destination societies, while the second potentially triggers complex reconfigurations of social positions across ethnoracial groups. To illustrate these broad dynamics, I will rely heavily on specific examples from the US case. The focus on the United States is due to two factors. First, American society combines a long history of strongly established "racial order" with constant immigration from various geographic origins; it thus constitutes a powerful laboratory that allows us to study the variation in the interplay between migration and ethnoracial inequality. Second, the ethnic and racial dimensions of inequality have been studied extensively in the United States and documented in empirical social sciences inquiry; the American literature therefore offers rich empirical materials. Although one may find some similarities in the combination of ethnoracial and migration components in many national European contexts, interpretations in terms of ethnoracial dynamics are rarer in Europe, in part because European countries generally refrain from presenting themselves as "racialized" societies.[10] When possible, I will nonetheless discuss some historical or contemporary situations that hint at such dynamics in the European context.

Fitting in the ethnoracial order
Migrants enter destination societies characterized by more or less salient ethnoracial classification systems, and they mobilize, individually and/or collectively, a wide range of resources while negotiating the ways in which they *fit within* these systems. In their investigations of the trans-formation of the contours of whiteness at the turn of the twentieth century in the United States, historians have documented the "struggle" of Italians, Jews, Irish, and other immigrant groups to achieve their classification as white. The working of these "whites of a different color" (Jacobson 1999) toward full whiteness benefited from a particular demographic context (the sharp decrease in migration flows at the time) and from overall favorable conditions in terms of social mobility (Massey 1995). But their whitening also derived from specific self-identification

strategies characterized by a strong distancing from African Americans (Ignatiev 1995; Foner 2005; Roediger 2005). While the European migrant trajectory was traditionally analyzed in the sociology of immigration as a success story of immigrant assimilation, contemporary research tends to more accurately portray it as an example of "boundary shifting." Boundary shifting metaphorically refers to the translation of a boundary, collectively incorporating certain out-group members without altering the very meaning of the boundary or its salience within social relations. The full incorporation of European migrants in the white category was thus mainly driven by the expansion in the meaning of this category. In their attempts to reconcile the classical approaches of immigrant assimilation with these ethnoracial boundary perspectives, Alba and Nee conceive boundary shifting as a particular mode of "immigrant assimilation" (2003: 60–1). Some scholars nonetheless emphasize the dissonances between boundary shifting dynamics and assimilation perspectives. While, according to the latter, migrants are supposed to converge over time and across generations toward the mainstream in destination societies, mainly as a result of social mobility and acculturation, the recent exploitation of longitudinal historical data tends to invalidate this type of trajectory for European migration at the turn of the twentieth century in the United States. Recent research using linked census data shows that these groups did not experience initial labor market disadvantages; Abramitzky and colleagues (2014) did not even find a significant initial gap between the wages of immigrants and natives. Analyses in this vein stress the crucial role of ethnoracial classification mechanisms, involving the self-distancing of European migrant communities from African American minorities (with the central example of the Irish), but also that of local states as well as the federal state, which quickly considered these migrants as white (Fox et al. 2012). Thus, rather than attenuating the white/non-white ethnoracial boundaries, the whitening of European migrants provides an example of the "ethnoracial-boundary-rigidication effect" of migration. In other terms, contrary to the immigration diversification paradigm, the extension of the domain of whiteness in the early twentieth century in the United States has led to the reinforcement of the color line, leading to the consolidation of the specific form of US anti-black racial domination.

Migrants may use several resources to *fit up*. One of the most documented resources is the instrumental use of citizenship. The racialized conception of "white citizenship" created a space for the whitening of European migrants (Fox and Bloemraad 2015). Similar dynamics took place in postcolonial France with the "repatriation" of "return colonials" from Algeria. Although a considerable share of them were born and grew up in colonial Algeria, the racialized characteristic of French citizenship within colonial French history was definitely a resource they used to integrate into the French mainstream upon migration (Couto 2013). The instrumentalization of citizenship in the negotiation of one's position in the ethnoracial order has also been at work for French overseas migrants as a strategy to reduce the classification potency of their skin color and facilitate their incorporation into the French mainstream (Haddad 2018). Commonwealth migration in the UK offers similarly interesting insights on the relation between migration, ethnoraciality, and citizenship (Hansen 2000). And beyond citizenship, other resources such as legal status, language, religion, and skin color may also be sources of instrumentalization in this struggle for classification as a way for migrants to distance themselves from disadvantaged minorities. In that sense, the racial attitudes of migrants themselves and the ways in which they affect attitudes of those who stay back home are a fruitful area of inquiry and participate in shaping racial dynamics (Roth and Kim 2013). Research in the United States shows that immigrants have significantly more negative views toward blacks than those born in the US and migration might transfer these anti-black attitudes transnationally.

While the whitening of European migrants has been frequently presented as a success story, migrants' strategies and struggles for categorization do not always pay off. Indeed, working toward *fitting up* is constrained by a variety of structural factors. The comparison of two pioneering studies conducted by Waters powerfully illustrates the constraints in the flexibility of ethnoracial categorization and the barriers that hinder their instrumentalization by migrant groups. While in *Ethnic Options* (1990), Waters shows that the descendants of European migration of the beginning of the century managed to couple their whitening with some degree of "ethnic diversity," mobilizing the specificity of their origin or ancestry in a situational, instrumental, and optional way, research conducted by the same sociologist on West Indian migrants reveals that their "ethnic options" are much more limited (Waters 1999). While first-generation West Indians emphasize the specificity of their national/geographic origin as a strategy to distance themselves from the African American group (mainly drawing on differences in the meaning of skin color categorizations in the Caribbean and US contexts), they do not succeed in resisting their assignation, and that of their children, to the US understanding of blackness. The evolution of their ethnoracial identification across the generations indicates a *"fitting down"* dynamic. This form of downward classification of migrants into stigmatized minority groups recalls the concept forged by Portes and colleagues of "segmented assimilation" (Portes and Zhou 1993; Portes and Rumbaut 2001).

All in all, even though the segment of the ethnoracial order into which they fit is uncertain, underlining the need for a case-to-case study of migrant ethnoracial categorization, these examples commonly highlight eventual stability and even, in some cases, rigidification of the existing ethnoracial order in situations of migration. In other words, migrant groups might fit up or down the ethnoracial hierarchy depending on the interplay of the assignation and self-identification elementary processes, but they ultimately *fit in* the order and do not challenge its symbolic organization (i.e., its hierarchy) nor its effectiveness in biasing the distribution of resources. In this sense, their assimilation takes a conservative meaning; migration gets absorbed into existing ethnoracial categorizations.

Reshaping the ethnoracial order

Some population projections in the United States highlight the transformation of ethnoracial boundaries in the country as a result of sustained migration turning the white majority into a minority. This underlines that migration changes the ethnoracial order mechanically, in an arithmetic way, by adding "non-majority" types of people. A similar line of argument about the demographic potency of migration is used when it comes to intermarriages and their ethnoracial mixing effects. While sustained migration has certainly changed the demographics of the United States, whether this is sufficient in itself to change the ethnoracial order is not so straightforward. Essentially, if the principles of human classification in ethnoracial categories remain stable, the future white quantitative minority may remain a white qualitative majority and the racial order will persist unchallenged. In other words, the transformative potential of migration not only resides in its capacity to change the "raw materials" on which human ethnoracial classifications build; it also goes through changes in the positioning of these materials in the ethnoracial order (Hochschild et al. 2012).

Rather than fitting in, migrant groups may work toward the creation of new categorical positions in the ethnoracial order. One common strategy consists in refusing to be classified in existing categories, building on the discrepancy between the perception and interpretation of racialized markers in the origin and destination countries. Ethnographic research documents the intrinsic difficulty of some migrants' self-classification in the US ethnoracial system; Mexicans, Brazilians, New Indians, Puerto Ricans, and African blacks are the most studied in the literature.

Historically, Mexican migrants to the United States have posed important classification issues. A distinct Mexican category was added to the race census question in 1930; the evolution of Mexicans' classification then took some quite chaotic directions, with indications that they should be classified as whites followed by considerable self-classification in the "other" category (Rodriguez 2000; Hochschild and Powell 2008). This played an important role in Mexicans' resistance to fitting into the US racial order, as they drew on the argument that they might equally mark the black or the white category (in a context where census racial categorization was exclusive), and they mobilized for the introduction of a separate Hispanicity question. Research highlights the "struggle for categorization" that the separation between the race and the Hispanicity questions entails in the United States, with the aim of expanding the domain of whiteness to Central and South American migrants, at least as an option for self-identification (Choldin 1986; Rodriguez 2000; Yancey 2003; Morning 2005; Schor 2017). Similar lines of interpretation emerge in the case of the debate over a potential Arab American census category, primarily driven by their discomfort with existing available categories (Ajrouch and Jamal 2007; Tehranian 2010). This boundary work toward additional categories does not only "nominally" change the categorization; it is capable of reshaping the hierarchy underlying it. The establishment of a non-white Hispanic category triggers dynamics of triangulation of the American racial order, diverging from the dialectic nature of the black/white color line (Bonilla-Silva 2004; Frank et al. 2010). This example clearly shows that the introduction of new categories is capable of changing the relation between existing ones, opening space for new divisions or new coalitions (Abascal 2015).

Moreover, rather than adding new categories, migration may introduce heterogeneity within existing ethnoracial categorization by rendering some "migration-related" distinctions salient within groups. In the United States, continual flows of migration since the 1960s have created what Massey calls "complex ethnicity" (1995: 645). This "migration replenishment" introduced new lines of separation within the same ethnoracial group according to nativity (or immigrant generation), period of arrival, and length of stay (Kasinitz et al. 2002; Waters and Jiménez 2005; Jiménez 2008). Boundaries can even be reconfigured within groups of the same national origin, as shown in the case of Mexican immigrants (Jiménez 2008). Wimmer (2013) describes similar patterns of divisions between old and new migrants in Switzerland. Migration thus creates divisions within existing ethnoracial categories that arise out of the heterogeneity of migratory trajectories and their changing contexts; in some configurations this may lead to a shift in categories of identification in favor of migratory-driven identification (old versus new migrants; first- versus second-generation migrants).

Transformation of the racial order occurs not only by the production of "new categories" or the creation of subdivisions in existing ethnoracial categories; it might also consist of diluting the correlation between ethnoracial categories and social attainment outcomes. In other terms, migration may directly affect the mapping of inequality into ethnoracial categories. These dynamics take place when migrants retain different associations between clear-cut, categorizable markers in the host society and in socioeconomic resources. African migrants, for example, are straightforwardly categorized as blacks in the US (as a matter of fact, they tend to be "darker" than African Americans), while their experience of blackness is quite different from that of African Americans.[11] Moreover, most of these migrants are highly educated and quite successful in the labor market (Jasso 2011). This migration thus holds the potential to weaken the association between skin color and socioeconomic achievements in US society. If this type of migration becomes sizable and durable, it potentially constitutes a challenge to the general pattern of skin tone stratification in US society. Moreover, rather than lowering the equivalence of minority groups with social disadvantage, immigration is also capable of attenuating the association of the majority group with socioeconomic advantage. The socioeconomic success of Asian migrants, presented as a model minority in the United States but also in some European countries, potentially "recasts" the traditional relationship between ethnoraciality and achievement (Jiménez and Horowitz 2013; Xu and Lee 2013). These insights clearly hint at migration's potentialities of destabilizing and reshaping the ethnoracial order.

Since the pioneering work of Bauböck (1998) and Zolberg and Woon (1999), followed by Alba and Nee (2005) and Wimmer (2013), the concept of boundary work has been increasingly used in the literature, supplementing the traditional assimilation framework, or at least highlighting its ethnoracial dimension. On the whole, the body of research reviewed above points to the subversive dimension in the effect of migration on ethnoracial inequality and questions the "benign" representations of immigrant assimilation. Destabilizing the ethnoracial status quo entails strategies, struggles, and mobilization and also diverse forms of resistance, opposition, and backlash. This results in a wide variation in the directions and outcomes of boundary work in the context of migration. The currently flourishing scholarship that studies the fluidity of "ethnoracial categorization" highlights the fact that its permeability varies along gender, socioeconomic attainment, marital status, place of residence, phenotypic characteristics, etc. (Saperstein and Penner 2012; Liebler et al. 2017). Analyses drawing on individual longitudinal data in particular have powerfully contributed to our knowledge of these individual dynamics of ethnoracial formation in situations of migration. The decisive impact of skin color on the ethnoracial classification of Latino groups in the United States (Golash-Boza 2006; Golash-Boza and Darity 2008; Telles and Ortiz 2008) suggests that their absorption into a wide "non-white minority" group is a more likely scenario than racial triangulation (Gans 1999; Bonilla-Silva 2004; Massey 2009; Fox and Guglielmo 2012; Lichter 2013).

Along with these individual factors, macro factors such as the salience of pre-existing racial categories, their historical relations to migration, and the strength of their correlation with the distribution of resources may also affect the classification of migrant groups. In the United States, the historical thickness of the black/white color line translates into a certain "comparative advantage" conferred upon immigrant minorities, especially when they manage to organize and mobilize for ethnic/social capital (Lieberson 1981; Waldinger 1995; Kasinitz 2008). Conversely, some authors insist that the civil rights legacy and the fact that immigrant minorities benefited from the African American struggle increase their likelihood of identifying with the "dominated group" (Smith 2005a, 2005b).

These ethnoracial boundary-making dynamics are also shown to be sensitive to variability in the context of interaction between individuals and groups. This speaks in favor of an extension in the levels of analysis rather than the predominance of a unique observational scale – with the host country level disproportionately assumed to be the most relevant. As with cultural processes in general, local contexts of interaction (e.g., families, schools, firms, neighborhoods, cities, regions) produce specific meanings for ethnoracial categorizations, affecting their consequences for individual actions in these contexts and sometimes beyond. In large countries, the interpretation of ethnoracial categories and their implications in social life varies across distinct institutional or regional contexts such as states or other types of administrative entities (see, e.g., Loewen 1971; Leonardo 1984; Marrow 2011). And even in a smaller national context, some differences still exist across urban settings, or between urban and rural areas, leading to different patterns of migrants' incorporation across these areas. This necessary contextualization of ethnoracial meaning-making nevertheless does not contradict the relevance of macro-level perspectives that insist on the impact of migration on the global schemes of human classification, a discussion I will explore further below (Banton 1977, 1998; Collins 2001).

Migration and global ethnoracial reconfigurations

The transnational aspect of migration causes the scope of its effects to transcend the perimeter of the nation-state, potentially affecting global ethnoracial systems of categorization. Similar to what I described above as the ethnoracial order of societies, global processes of human categorizations are tied to the macro dynamics of resource distribution sustaining a "global ethnoracial order." One of the most salient "global ethnoracial orders" consists of the classification of humans in terms of nationalities; I will refer to this nationality-based classification as "international classification." I will discuss below how migration contributes to redefining the "nation" in the nation-state, with likely effects on the international classification. I will then focus on migration's potential for triggering trans-national ethnoracial reconfigurations that destabilize the international classification.

Redefining the nation in nation-state

The modern conception of citizenship is intrinsically "ethnic"; even within the most liberal *jus soli* states, the rules of citizenship are tied to birthright (Joppke 2010). The organization of the worldwide population as citizens of nation-states relies on an "international classification" that emerged in the eighteenth and nineteenth centuries, covering the planet's population in the twenty-first century.[12] This international classification is a specific type of ethnoracial categorization that is coupled with claims for self-governance and independence, endorsed formally by state legal and military apparatuses. In other words, nation-states are specific forms of ethnoracial "groups." This relatively recent type of ethnoracial categorization derives from global ethnoracial formation processes that, similar to those described above within nations, mainly consist of making (national) meaning out of human differences. While nation-building has frequently drawn on genealogic (and even biologic) communalities (encapsulated in the idea of peoplehood), meaning-making processes mostly derive from historic narratives, "collective memories," and other forms of ethnic attributes on which the distinctiveness of a nation is built (Anderson 1983; Mongia 2018).

This international classification has been increasingly correlated with the distribution of resources at the global level. As shown by Milanovic (2016), between-country inequality has been sharply increasing throughout the nineteenth and twentieth centuries, hand in hand with the building and consolidation of nation entities. While the trends of global inequality include a myriad of economic, demographic, political, and military factors, the effectiveness of social categorization in biasing resource distribution is an important underlying mechanism. The categorical creation of nations has reinforced within-nation closure (taking the form of the welfare state, yet with huge variations in its roles and means across nations). While the welfare state has definitely been an "internal" equalizer, it has also proceeded by external "opportunity hoarding" at the global level. Thus, the generalization of nation-state building across the planet has progressively attenuated inequality within nations, increasing inequality across them.

In a similar vein to its effects within societies, migration reshapes this global ethnoracial order embedded in international classification because it consists in the circulation of national members across nation-states. By crossing their formal borders, migrants potentially affect the meaning-making processes surrounding the cultural boundaries of these entities.

One of the most striking effects of migration concerns the "national bounding" of countries. By provoking the settlement of extra-territorial, non-citizen, and potentially "culturally" different others in the nation-state, migration disrupts the "ideal-typical" model of the latter, which draws heavily on an integrated conception of territoriality, citizenry, and culture (Brubaker 2010). As pointed out in Chapter 4, this perspective leads to the inversion of the well-established tradition in sociology and political sciences that relates immigrants' modes of integration to a typology of citizenship models grounded in supposedly particular "cultures," "traditions," "histories," or "philosophies."[13] It stresses the capacity of migration to transform and reshape these national "narratives" (Joppke 1999; Vertovec 2011). Historians tend to agree upon the determinant effect of accelerated migration and mixing through which the world's population was considerably redistributed in the eighteenth and nineteenth centuries on the emergence of nations as forms of belonging. Noiriel (1988, 2001) offers a thorough analysis of the French case, the oldest country of immigration in Europe, stressing the role of migration and its increasing interpretation in terms of "foreignness" in the construction of Frenchness as a mark of national identity, thus provoking the decline of once-strong regional identities. In the United States, the use of migration in the construction of nationhood took quite a different direction, emphasizing the immigrant foundations of the nation and integrating it into the "national narratives." While France is undoubtedly a "country of immigrants," it is not, unlike the United States, a "nation of immigrants." These differences in the role of immigration in the foundational national narratives of France and the United States took shape despite demographic and historical similarities in patterns and trends of populations inflows. Analysis along similar lines has been conducted on British nation-building (Paul 1997). While the central role of immigration in nation-state building is extremely apparent in "classic immigration countries" (Freeman 1995) – that is, Canada, the United States, New Zealand, Australia – it can also be detected in countries all around the world; Argentina, Brazil, and Malaysia are among the most studied in this respect.

The effects of migration on the meaning of nations reach further than just the first stages of nation-state building. It continues to impact their institutionalization via various legal and administrative logistics, as discussed in Chapter 4, solidifying and perpetuating the symbolic separation between nationals and aliens. With the immediate assigning of immigrants to the non-national out-group, the sense of belonging to the national group becomes increasingly shaped in opposition (or at least in reaction) to migration. By situating migrants outside the nation, the administrative management of immigration enhances non-immigrants' self-identification in terms of nativity, "indigenousness," or majority (Waldinger 2003; Jacobs and Rea 2005; Bail 2008). Banton (1983) described this dialectic related to the construction of a majority group while assigning individuals to a minority group in terms of "minus-one" ethnicity (see also Guillaumin 1985). In other terms, migration is central in the interplay between self- and assigned identifications in the formation of national boundaries. There is thus a sort of intrinsic racialization in the state categorization of individuals into citizens and foreigners, with ramifications that extend far beyond the legal dimension (Goldberg 2002; Anderson 2013). This leads to immigration policies being deeply implicated in the making and maintaining of racial differences. In the United States, research shows that migration at the turn of the twentieth century exacerbated racial meanings – in particular white normativity – within the American national identity (Fox 2012). In a similar vein, some scholars argue that immigration is currently reinforcing "essentialized" understandings of national identities in many European countries. Recent reforms in immigration and integration laws clearly illustrate this trend, increasingly dictating a form of "cultural" or "civic" integration, with particular emphasis on the necessity for migrants to embrace the host country's history, language, traditions, and institutions. In France, these policies have particularly glorified French-style secularism (*laïcité*) as well as the commitment to "Western" standards of gender equality (Safi 2014). The assumption that these cultural values and norms are homogeneously shared by the nationals contributes not only to some migrants – particularly those with a Muslim background, in the case of France as well as many other European countries – being designated as "foreign," but also to the endorsement of an essentialized connotation of Frenchness (Lorcerie 2007; Simon and Escafré-Dublet 2009). From this point of view, "French republicanism" has been functioning as a powerful cultural "repertoire," feeding an immigrant/French categorization that is increasingly influential in reshaping the dynamics of social inequality in France (Lamont 2000). In line with FitzGerald's (2017) insights in his history of racialized citizenship, the French case confirms that *jus soli* is fully compatible with a racialized citizenship, especially in postcolonial states. Beaman (2015) mobilizes the concept of "cultural citizenship" to describe this ongoing boundary work that is redefining the frontiers of Frenchness in reaction to migration.

Consequently, migration potentially transforms the process of ethnoracial meaning-making that surrounds national identity within states. From this perspective, paradoxically, and contrary to the "romantic" representation of migration as a postnational driving force, international migration has in fact been contributing to the consolidation of the global ethnoracial categorization that consists in classifying the world's inhabitants into culturally meaningful "nations." These dynamics might also reinforce national-meaning in the home country, as some diasporas may forge "nationalistic" networks. This is shown to be the case of Turkish immigrants in France and Germany, for example (Kastoryano 2002, 2006). In short, these "nationalistic" backlashes consolidate and sometimes sharpen national boundaries, increasing their potency in shaping the global "ethnoracial order."

Nonetheless, by decoupling place of residency from place of birth, migration-induced identity dynamics also hold the potential to destabilize and reshape the global ethnoracial order, triggering negotiations for alternative systems of human categorization that are situated at the transnational level.

Migration and ethnoracial formation processes beyond national categories
In addition to the effects of migration on ethnoracial formation processes that shape the national bounding of host countries and the categorization of populations within them, migration's effects on ethnoracial categorization may take place at the *transnational level*.

First, as a consequence of the transnational nature of migrant mobility, country-specific ethnoracial categorizations become mobile. In other words, ethnoracial meanings also migrate, actually "carried" by migrants themselves (Lorcerie 2010; Roth 2012; Waldinger 2015). In that sense, migration has the potential to weaken the specificity of national settings in the meaning-making process surrounding human markers. In a study of how Puerto Rican and Dominican migrants contribute to the importation to and diffusion of the dichotomous view of race prevailing in the United States in their home countries, characterized by the prevalence of more continuous racial classifications, Roth (2012) describes the migration of the ethnoracial categorizations themselves. These dynamics of "cultural translation" are enhanced by the cultural dimensions of current globalization dynamics. Studies on migrant transnationalism contribute significantly to our understanding of these phenomena of cultural transfer between categorization systems caused at least in part by migration. In the sociological and anthropological literature, transnational perspectives have indeed been highlighting the social remittances involved in migration. These remittances actually include ethnoracial meanings and classifications (Levitt 2001; Zamora 2016). In this respect, migration may enhance a shared meaning of ethnoracial categories across nation-state borders.

And more generally, beyond the home–host country dynamics, migration feeds the reconfigurations of global ethnoracial categorization. As pointed out by theorists of race, there is an intrinsic global dimension to racial formation, closely related to large-scale historical processes such as imperialism, slavery, and colonization, with worldwide implications for the categorization of human beings (Said 1978; Quijano 2000; Winant 2001; Fredrickson 2002; Goldberg 2002; Wallerstein and Balibar 2007; Emirbayer and Desmond 2015; Mongia 2018). These macro-level processes of ethnoracial formation have in fact played crucial roles in state-building and the creation of nationality as an identification category (Wallerstein 1984; Wimmer and Min 2006). They continue to feed the global cultural repertoires that fuel the ethnoracial meaning-making processes. These macro approaches tend to move the field closer to global history and "international relations" – understood not only as country-level geopolitics but also more generally as a form of "human geopolitics" (Collins 1999; Winant 2001; Wihtol de Wenden 2010; FitzGerald et al. 2014). Systems of domination between regions and countries and human groups continue to feed worldwide negotiations of ethnoracial meanings, contributing to the cultural repertoires invested in the multilevel spaces of ethnoracial formation. Commonly used classifications that proceed by the allocation of individuals and groups to large-scale transnational categories, including those that refer to more or less institutionalized boundaries (Europe, the West, the global South, postcolonial countries, etc.), should be understood as emanating from these global processes of ethnoracial formation. While authors who develop these approaches tend to use the word "race" more often than "ethnicity" (in expressions such as the global race politics, global race theory, the world racial system), these transnational spaces of ethnoracial meaning-making are not particularly distinct from what I describe below as elementary mechanisms of ethnoracial formation, and may be included as one component of this general process. Macro-level ethnoracial categorizations also emanate from identity assignment and self-identification of individuals to groups and therefore affect and interact with local and national levels of ethnoracial formation. They also map the distribution of resources globally, thus forming a global ethnoracial order.

Migration has a prominent role in the paths these global processes of ethnoracial formation may take. First, by creating "real spheres" of interactions in destination countries between migrants coming from different national contexts, migration may render salient cross-national commonalities such as religions, phenotypes, historical experiences, etc., which potentially destabilizes the ubiquity of the international classification. In other words, migration creates an avenue for regrouping national-ities into aggregated categories, leading to transnational categories of identity. Research has, for instance, described the ways in which the experience of migration from diverse countries of Central or South America to the United States has contributed to the shaping of pan-national belonging or "panethnicity" (Roth 2009; Mora 2014). Similar dynamics are also described for the Asian panethnicity (Okamoto 2014). Hispanicity, endorsed as an official census category, is not the only available aggregated classi-fication; Jamaican migrants tend to identify with West Indian or black labels (Waters 1999). Hyphenated national categorizations are also shown to be an identity option in US research (Rumbaut 1994; Feliciano 2009). The recon-figuration of ethnoracial categories is not limited to simply grouping national categories; cross-national markers such as religion, skin color, and language that share ethnoracial meaning across national boundaries may also be invested within these dynamics (Espiritu 1992; Basch et al. 1994; Fouron and Glick Schiller 2002; Levitt 2003; Haller and Landolt 2005; Kastoryano 2006). This investment may consolidate a sort of social capital that translates into group closure within economic, associative, political, or social organizations (Faist 2000; Kasinitz and Vickerman 2001; Portes et al. 2002). Moreover, panethnic reconfigurations are not limited to the host society; they may be extended transnationally to migrant sending societies (Roth 2009). This strand of research contributes to reconceptualizing transnationalism as linkages to a collective identity in formation in the context of migration, and therefore as a "type of consciousness" (Vertovec 1999) or new "ways of belonging" (Levitt and Schiller 2004). Most of these identity reconfigurations are only measurable in long-term investigations and across generations.

These boundary-making processes are also shown to be related to common experiences in the host societies. Here again, a form of "transnational racism" (Castles 2005), which affects migrants in host societies in a lasting manner across generations, may trigger a sense of belonging to transnational categories of identification based on skin color, religion, or broad geographic or third world origins. These dynamics hint at a transnational or universal dimension of minorities' struggle for ethnoracial recategorization (Goldberg 2009). Such reconfigurations do not only concern disadvantaged groups, however; they may also be at work within the dominant group. North–South migration may contribute to the reconfiguration of Westernness/whiteness. Ethnographic research describes clear-cut hierarchies of migrants in massive immigration countries such as the Arab Gulf, where Western migrants and global South migrants (mostly South Asians) experience sharp differences in the economic, legal, and symbolic conditions of migration (Jamal 2015; Cosquer 2018; Le Renard 2019).

These accounts of ethnoracial boundary-making located at the transnational level emphasize the ways in which migration creates real situations of interactions across international classification categories, potentially opening space for the negotiation of alternative schemes of categorization. They invite us to move beyond the well-established categories of migration analysis, such as countries and nationalities of origin. Attempts at cross-national ethnic, racial, or cultural classification may be understood as operating in this direction despite the considerable anthropological and historical debates that surround them (Heath et al. 2016).

* * *

The diverse body of research reviewed in this chapter highlights the extent to which migration affects the current ethnoracial order at the border of nation-states, within their societies and worldwide. In contrast to the international division of labor and legal categorization, in which mechanisms of inequality endogenously relate human categorization and resource distribution, the migration/ ethnoracial formation nexus emphasizes the role of "external" or "exogenous" categorization processes that are situated at the symbolic and intersubjective level. In addition to their categorization as "types of workers" and "types of citizens," ethnoracial formation categorizes migrants as "types of humans." If the intersection between these three channels of the migration effect on inequality produces overlapping areas that are very frequently assessed in the empirical literature (ethnoracial discrimination in the labor market, racialization of immigration laws), it remains analytically useful to stress essential differences between the three channels. Unlike the global division of labor and legal categorization, the ethnoracial channel is not intrinsically tied to the distribution of resources and does not systematically lead to social disadvantage. National and transnational dynamics of ethnoracial categorization indeed imply that migrants neither arrive equally in a host country (as they are previously "sorted" according to existing ethnoracial schemes) nor evolve equally within it (since the combination of assignment/self-identification exerts a wide variety of effects on the outcome of ongoing ethnoracial categorizations, with disparate results in terms of access to resources). Ethnoracial formation dynamics in situations of migration are affected by relational and organizational contexts and by the political mobilization of groups and individuals negotiating the social meaning attributed to ethnoracial categories. The processes of negotiation, contestation, and legitimization of ethnoracial categories give rise to complex configurations that result in heterogeneous outcomes across groups. This leaves room for some "uncertainty" in the degree to which their effect on inequality becomes durable, reproducible, potentially corrigible, or even reversible. This uncertainty captures, at least in part, the heterogeneity observed between the socioeconomic destinies of immigrant groups. In this sense, immigrants do not uniformly become "ethnoracial minorities" in host societies.

There is also another source of "uncertainty" in the migration/ethnoracial formation/inequality nexus. It is related to the contingency of ethnoracial markers and the variability of their meaning across social settings. Because migration potentially brings about "new materials" and new interpretations of existing materials, the matching of migrant groups' characteristics with existing categorization gives rise to a wide variety of possibilities, which renders the directions that ethnoracial reconfiguration can take difficult to predict. Thus, while the unequal nature of the global division of labor and legal categorization may seem immediate, the relation between migration, ethnoracial formation, and social inequality calls for more nuances.

Finally, despite this uncertainty surrounding the relation between migration, ethnoracial formation, and social inequality, this channel is paradoxically the one that carries the most lasting impacts. While economic and legal inequalities may be transmitted to the second generations (and possibly beyond), they most often do so following mainstream social reproduction mechanisms. In both these channels, the original mechanisms of inequality (import of labor, legal and administrative categorization) mainly concern those who migrated across labor markets or institutionalized nation-states – that is, first-generation migrants. Conversely, the self-identification and assignment elementary processes at stake in the ethnoracial channel are not first-generation specific; they may reproduce, keep going and also transform across migrant generations (Feliciano and Rumbaut 2018). This may explain the fact that assimilation trends expected to be measured across generations for immigrants' outcomes diverge considerably according to ethnoracial background. In other words, the ethnoracial channel potentially creates racialized assimilation pathways for migrants and their descendants in host societies. The ethnoracial channel thus potentially enhances the durability of migration-driven inequality.

Conclusion:
Migration, an Issue of
Social Justice

While a glance at historical trends in massive migration is enough to reveal the inaccuracy of thinking about contemporary population movements only in terms of demographic pressure, it is undeniable that international migration exerts a growing political pressure on the national, the international, and the global scale.

More than a century of social science research reviewed in this book shows how cross-country migration has been a significant factor in local and global social transformations, with implications in terms of power relations and resource distribution. Migratory flows are not only intrinsically related to worldwide unbalanced demographic, economic, and political contexts; they also have the potential to reshape these multidimensional patterns of inequality within or between countries as well as globally, across the earth's inhabitants. Drawing on a multidisciplinary literature, I have identified three channels through which migration affects the dynamics of social inequality. The migration of humans reshapes the distribution of economic and political resources by categorizing workers (global division of labor) and citizens (legal categorization). Migration also affects group boundary-making by provoking situations of symbolic (re)classification along ethnoracial lines. In each of these channels, migration exerts distinct categorization power that directly impacts inequality dynamics. Beyond geographic mobility, migrants may consequently be conceived as *types of workers, types of citizens*, and *types of humans* in contemporary social stratification regimes. These three mechanisms of inequality related to migration are inherently transnational. The global division of labor and the legal processes of migrant categorization both go beyond the perception of the nation-state as the societal "container": the former draws on a global framing of class-based inequality and the latter shows how cross-national citizenship categories intrinsically derive from cross-border population movements. As for the effect of migration on the dynamics of ethnoracial formation, it relates to processes of social construction of race and ethnicity that unfold at the national, subnational, and transnational levels. Migration is thus a major dimension of worldwide power relations; conceptualizing it as a case-study of inequality bridges the gap between research focused on within-country inequality and scholarship concerned with global inequality. This approach also helps counter the immediate association in the political debate between immigration, on the one hand, and national "problems," on the other, which fundamentally draws on the supposed externality and exogeneity of population cross-border movements. Re-centering the debate on migration around issues of inequality and social justice is capable of changing the predominant narratives in public policy discussions. But reframing the narrative is not enough; institutional change is also crucial. Beyond the regulation and management of human flows, solving the "problem" of international migration also requires the conception and implementation of trans-state egalitarian policies that combine redistribution and recognition in a way to address its economic, legal, and ethnoracial inequality channels.

Notes

Chapter 1: From National to Migration Societies

1 Manning (2013: 7) distinguishes three types: home-community migration, colonization, and whole-community migration.

2 In 2017, there were 193 member countries of the UN (not including Palestine and Vatican City/Holy See, which have the status of non-member observers). This number has changed dramatically and regularly since the creation of the UN in 1945 (with 51 founding members). The UN defines a migrant as "any person that changes his or her country of usual residence."

3 Paradoxically, measuring internal migration is more complex than measuring international migration, at least on a global level. Tentative estimations suggest that around 763 million people were living outside their region of birth in 2005. A five-year span is quite common in the measurement of internal migration; this leads to an estimate of 229 million people that were living within the same country in 2010 and 2005, but in a different region in 2005 (Bell and Charles-Edward 2013). Internal migration forms a major share of population dynamics in large countries such as India and China.

4 Here, I use a mainstream definition of migration that is widely accepted today both at the national and the international levels. There is nonetheless some variation in the applications of this definition in official population records across the world; apart from country of birth, criteria such as country of citizenship, purpose of visit or visa type, place of last permanent residence, and duration of stay are sometimes used. Some researchers argue for the integration of all forms of "transnational mobility," including cross-border travel and tourism, which have grown impressively in recent decades (Recchi et al. 2019). Moreover, it must be noted that the international migration approach has been criticized by scholars (mainly historians and geographers), who have shifted the lens toward "cultural" boundary-crossing rather than state-level boundaries. While there are undoubtedly intersections between the mainstream definition of international migration and other forms of geographic mobility, the institutionalization of state borders and the overlapping of geographic, political, and cultural factors that are involved in such mobility confer a specific status upon international migration (Lucassen and Lucassen 2014).

5 From the perspective of a home country c', emigrants are those who were born in c' but do not live there anymore at time t. This vision of migration, which focuses on the combination of home and host countries, tends to overshadow the stepwise and circular nature of many migration trajectories.

6 The latest estimations suggest that these two categories of migrants (return colonials and emigrants' children) form around 2 percent of the French population (Beauchemin et al. 2015).

7 Social stratification theory classically distinguishes between ascriptive (race, gender, age) and achieved status (education, occupation) (Parsons 1951). The former relates to inherited characteristics that are largely unchanging.

8 It is interesting to note that the perspective of the sending country would conversely consider an "emigrant status" as an achieved or chosen one.

9 This stable feature of the definition also applies from the perspective of the origin country: emigrants stay emigrants as long as they don't come back. A growing interest in return migration led the UN to define the notion: "Persons

returning to their country of citizenship after having been international migrants (whether short-term or long-term) in another country and who are intending to stay in their own country for at least a year." Estimations of return migration are imprecise: in OECD countries, 20 to 50 percent of migrants are expected to re-migrate within five years.

10 There is an ongoing debate on whether "migrant" or "refugee" should be used. These words have different connotations and are increasingly employed within specific ideological frames. "Migrant" is a generic term that designates persons who cross national boundaries. A refugee is a specific category of migrant defined in international law (the UN 1951 Convention on Refugees in Geneva) that provides international forced migrants with some rights ("non-refoulement," non-discriminatory social provisions, family reunification, etc.). The term "asylum seekers" refers to migrants who seek protection as refugees, and who apply for asylum in the country of destination (and whose claim for *refugee* status has not yet been assessed). Since the crisis at the time of writing is closely related to violence in Syria, Iraq, and other Middle Eastern countries, it mainly involves asylum seekers (who may potentially become refugees). It is noticeable nonetheless that the conventional distinctions between these terms become less operational in mass migration episodes.

11 More than 84 percent of the world's refugees live in low- and middle-income countries (UNHCR 2018).

12 "Assimilation is a process of interpretation and fusion in which persons and groups acquire the memories, sentiments, and attitudes of other persons and groups, and, by sharing their experience and history, are incorporated with them in a common cultural life" (Park and Burgess 1921: 735).

13 This straight line pattern of assimilation also applies to first generation migrants, whose acculturation is supposed to increase with length of stay in the host country.

14 The growing number of studies documenting the simultaneity of immigrant transnationalism and assimilation has increasingly led scholars to rethink their relations in conjunction rather than in opposition (Kivisto 2001; Levitt 2001; Morawska 2003).

15 For the most recent figures, see the IOM Missing Migrants Project: https://missingmigrants.iom.int/.
16 In OECD countries, the figures are estimated to be between 20 and 50 percent (OECD 2008).

Chapter 2: Migration and Elementary Mechanisms of Social Inequality: A Conceptual Framework

1 In social and political philosophy, equality is discussed as a normative concept grounded in the idea of justice (Rawls 1971; Sen 1980, 2009). This literature has greatly contributed to our understanding of whether and why equality is valuable and what kind of equality is important. Although being value-neutral about (in)equality is impossible, the approach in this book tends to be descriptive and does not discuss whether inequality is desirable, or fair, or whether it matters per se.
2 This distinction originated within the work of post-World War II social scientists such as Parsons (1951), Davis and Moore (1945). It was supposed to capture the difference between traits present at birth and attributes that are subsequently acquired. While sex and race are usually presented as prototypes of ascriptive processes, and education or occupation as prototypes of achieved positions, social scientists nowadays tend to agree that this distinction is much more valid in the perception of actors than it is in the nature of these attributes per se. In most modern societies, educational and other socioeconomic attainments are at least partly inherited and thus ascribed, while some dimensions of race and gender can be performed and achieved. The distinction is still useful nonetheless, because it emphasizes differences in the cultural essentialization of individual attributes. Differences in the degree of essentialization of attributes have sociocognitive implications that make them more or less resilient to social change and central to inequality dynamics.
3 According to Wright (1997: 11): "Genocide is thus always a potential strategy for non-exploitative oppressors. It is not an option in a situation of economic exploitation

because exploiters require the labor of the exploited for their material well-being."

4 For details, see Ridgeway (2001), Hogg and Ridgeway (2003), as well as other contributions in the volume edited by Hogg and Tindale (2001).

5 Relational mechanisms refer to all that may affect the probability of encounter and the modes of interaction between individuals. It is during these interactional situations that the social sense of the categories is likely to be renegotiated and/or some resources are likely to be distributed more or less unevenly. While Lamont and colleagues (2014) relate spatial processes to resource distribution processes, it seems to me that the distribution of individuals in space can be linked to a process of categorization (that of spaces themselves) and a process of resource distribution (space resources). Thus, just as is the case for the labor market, spatial divisions proceed both by categorization and distribution of resources. For a recent analytical approach on spatial inequality, see Galster and Sharkey (2017).

6 A discussion of these debates relating to cases of gender inequality may be found in the work of Ridgeway and Correll (2000, 2006).

Chapter 3: The Economic Channel: Migrant Workers in the Global Division of Labor

1 It is notable that migration is still tied to contemporary forms of slavery, as shown by the case of migrants from sub-Saharan Africa captured and sold as slaves in Libya (the CNN video that provoked international outrage clearly shows an auctioneer selling migrant men he describes as "big strong boys": https://edition.cnn.com/2017/11/14/africa/libya-migrant-auctions/index.html). While there is some disagreement on the definition of contemporary slavery, current estimations range around 40 million enslaved individuals worldwide. Although most of these different forms of "forced workers" (including victims of sex trafficking and child labor) are concentrated in

countries such as Mauritania and India, the figures remain shockingly high in developed countries where modern slavery seems to be closely tied to international migration, particularly its undocumented subset (see: https://www. washingtonpost.com/news/worldviews/wp/2013/10/17/ this-map-shows-where-the-worlds-30-million-slaves-live-there-are-60000-in-the-u-s/?noredirect=on&utm_term=. e4bb6ff9dcfe).

2 In Wallerstein's famous theoretical model, the semiperi-phery is supposed to fluidify the exploitative relations between the core and the periphery (Wallerstein 1974, 1984). World-system theory emphasizes the necessity to apply the within-nation approach to social stratification and inequality between countries. World-system research tradi-tionally considers the reproduction of economic inequality and class hierarchies as resulting from states occupying a particular world-system position.

3 Here, it must be noted that research on attitudes toward immigration finds little support for the economic compe-tition hypothesis (natives who are the most exposed to migrant competition in the labor market would be the most hostile to migration). All in all, this scholarship assesses the crucial role of education as a predictor of support for immigration. According to Hainmueller and Hopkins (2014), the education effect is less related to "self-interested concerns about wages" than it is to differences in cultural values and beliefs about immigration's socio-tropic impacts (mainly affecting the labor market and the economy).

4 See also the study by Peri et al. (2015), which uses variation in a US visa program that is specifically designed for high-skilled migrants employed in the STEM sector. Their findings show significant wage gains for natives, in particular the college-educated.

5 Of course, more nuanced lines of argument have been developed within the Marxist tradition. Miles's work on the racialization of migrant labor, a concept he uses with the aim of distinguishing between categorization and distribution involved in migrant labor, is one of the most elaborated theoretical frameworks in this regard (1982, 1989, 1993).

Chapter 4: The Legal Channel: Immigration Law, Administrative Management of Migrants, and Civic Stratification

1 The concept of citizenship is multidimensional, and there is considerable variation in the way scholars define it. For example, Bloemraad and colleagues (2008) distinguish four dimensions of citizenship: legal status, rights, political participation, and sense of belonging. Beaman (2016) highlights the cultural dimension of citizenship. Other accounts include gender, sexuality, ecology, etc.

2 Article 13 of the Universal Declaration of Human Rights recognizes the right to migration, i.e. the right to leave a country, including one's country of birth. Nonetheless, the article does not acknowledge a right of "immigration" or the right to enter a country.

3 For example, the EU budget for the management of external borders, migration, and asylum has been significantly reinforced, reaching more than €34.9 billion for the 2021–7 period, compared to €13 billion for the period 2014–20 (EU 2018).

4 Most undocumented migration is actually driven by "unlawfulness" constructed within the country rather than at its borders: expired visas, rejected asylum seekers, etc. (Donato and Armenta 2011; Vickstrom 2014).

5 Even within the EU free movement category, there is a hierarchy of channels that tends to fluidify mobility for the high-skilled, rich, and ethnoracially advantaged EU members, while hindering migration of those who are stigmatized as "undesirable." The example of restriction, hostility, and even deportation of the EU citizen Roma migrants in Western European countries is emblematic in this regard. It clearly highlights the intertwining of the ethnic/racial category with legal migration categories, and more generally points to the politics of mobility within the European Union (Sigona and Trehan 2009; Fox et al. 2012; Fox 2013; Yıldız and De Genova 2018).

6 For the most recent figures, see the IOM Missing Migrants Project: https://missingmigrants.iom.int/.

7 One may alternatively argue that legal categorizations are constructed with the aim of facilitating the labor market exploitation of migrants or in response to labor market structure failures (see Chapter 3 for more details). If the economic and legal dimensions of inequality related to migration are intertwined, causal analyses that focus on the effect of reforms, new laws, or new categories suggest that the legal dimension exerts a form of autonomy. This literature is reviewed in the next section.

8 Some subcategories also exist within the EU member states category (Schengen-EU, Eurozone-EU, etc.). There is also a line of separation between Western European countries and Central and Eastern European countries that mainly use the language of "older" and "new" member states.

Chapter 5: The Ethnoracial Channel: Migration, Group Boundary-Making, and Ethnoracial Classification

1 Distinctive contributions, such as Brubaker (2009) and Wimmer (2013), have arguably asserted the logical priority of ethnicity over race in an effort to usher the field away from the ubiquity of the US case. And it is indeed the case that they opened the way to impressive comparative empirical approaches that have considerably enriched the field. These approaches, however, are mainly focused on tracing and characterizing *"ethnic boundary-making."* On the other hand, critical race theory tends to consider that "eliminating race obscures its trace" to quote from Lentin (2016). As I argue in the following pages, even if there are definitely some theoretical grounds for an analytical distinction between race and ethnicity, the focus on their role in the relation between immigration and inequality increases the scope of their conceptual overlap. I therefore choose to combine the use of these terms with the aim of increasing the effectiveness of theory-building focused on stratificationist effects of migration.

2 In my discussion of concepts, I rely on a diversity of approaches to race and ethnicity that cross both disciplinary and paradigmatic boundaries. For example, I mobilize

critical race theory as well as cognitive and social psychology when it is useful for my purpose. Since the main focus of this book is not on race and ethnicity, my discussion inevitably fails to address in depth the central controversies in this area. And since the level of political contention in this literature is high, I also deliberately avoid taking clear ideological and political positions. Given the purpose of this chapter, the objective of my conceptual discussion is to provide an analytical framework that will allow me to disentangle specific mechanisms to describe how migration affects ethnoracial inequalities.

3 Brubaker draws a similar conclusion by stating: "Rather than seek to demarcate precisely their respective spheres, it may be more productive to focus on identifying and explaining patterns of variation on these and other dimensions, without worrying too much about where exactly race stops and ethnicity begins" (2009: 28).

4 Empirical objectivation potentialities nonetheless vary across the markers that are invested in ethnoracial categorizations. While one may use linguistic methodologies to measure objective differences between languages (Desmet et al. 2009), distance is trickier to objectify when it comes to phenotypes, religions, or cultures. In other words, while it is possible not only to assess that two languages are different but also to measure the intensity of this difference using intrinsic features of the languages themselves, the distance between categories grounded in race, ethnicity, or religion usually uses indirect measures such as intermarriage, homophily, or geographic segregation.

5 According to Brubaker, the growing interdisciplinarity and dialogue between different theoretical approaches enhance the representation of ethnicity, race (and nationhood) as a "single integrated family of forms of cultural understanding, social organization, and political challenge "(Brubaker 2009: 22).

6 As mentioned in the previous chapter, I choose to include the identity dimension of citizenship in my elaboration on the effect of immigration on ethnoracial categorization. I will refer to this type of categorization as based on nationality, understood here in relation to the concept of "nationhood" beyond the formal political and legal status it entails.

7 It is useful here to recall that gender was also a principle for

discriminatory citizenship in most Western societies until the 1960s and is so still in many societies. And, of course, gender is a categorization that maps socioeconomic inequality, especially in the labor market.

8 Nor is migration by itself necessarily generating cultural diversity (in terms of norms, values etc.), since within-group variation in cultural norms may be higher than across groups (Desmet et al. 2017).

9 This famous debate, held in the Spanish city of Valladolid, discussed the moral and theological implications of the colonization of the Americas. There were opposing views on the human nature of the indigenous populations and their rights not to be enslaved.

10 One may add here that this is related to the fact that in European societies, racialization mostly occurred outside the mainland (in the empires), while racialization took shape within the US national context. This has considerable implications on race scholarship in Europe and the US (Connell 1997).

11 Through the individual trajectory of a young Nigerian woman in the United States, C. Ngozi Adichie (2013) subtly unfolds the specificity of the racialization of African migrants in the United States and its subjective consequences on these migrants.

12 Although the exact figures are difficult to assess precisely, there are currently many millions of stateless people in the world, according to the UNHCR. Statelessness is an emblematic example of the ongoing state-building process in the twenty-first century and its close relation with ethno-racial categorizations.

13 As highlighted by Manning (2013), these approaches to national identity downplay the connections among cases, which is one reason why scholars tend to neglect migration as a factor encouraging the construction of nations.

References

Abascal, M., 2015. Us and Them: Black-White Relations in the Wake of Hispanic Population Growth. *American Sociological Review*, 80 (4), 789–813.

Abbott, A., 2001. *Chaos of Disciplines*. Chicago: University of Chicago Press.

Abbott, A., 2003. La Description face à la temporalité. *In*: Giorgio, B., and Olivier de Sardan, J.-P., eds., *Pratiques de la description*. Paris: EHESS, 41–53.

Abramitzky, R., Boustan, L. P., and Eriksson, K., 2012. Europe's Tired, Poor, Huddled Masses: Self-Selection and Economic Outcomes in the Age of Mass Migration. *American Economic Review*, 102 (5), 1832–1856.

Abramitzky, R., Boustan, L. P., and Eriksson, K., 2014. A Nation of Immigrants: Assimilation and Economic Outcomes in the Age of Mass Migration. *Journal of Political Economy*, 122 (3), 467–506.

Abrego, L. J., 2011. Legal Consciousness of Undocumented Latinos: Fear and Stigma as Barriers to Claims-Making for First- and 1.5-Generation Immigrants. *Law & Society Review*, 45 (2), 337–369.

Acker, J., 2006. Inequality Regimes, Gender, Class, and Race in Organizations. *Gender and Society*, 20 (4), 441–464.

Adida, C. L., Laitin, D. D., and Valfort, M.-A., 2016. "One Muslim is Enough!" Evidence from a Field Experiment in France. *Annals of Economics and Statistics*, 121/122, 121–160.

Ajrouch, K. J., and Jamal, A., 2007. Assimilating to a White Identity: The Case of Arab Americans. *International Migration Review*, 41 (4), 860–879.

Akerlof, G. A., 1970. The Market for "Lemons": Quality Uncertainty and the Market Mechanism. *Quarterly Journal of Economics*, 84 (3), 488–500.

Akerlof, G. A., 2000. Economics and Identity. *Quarterly Journal of Economics*, 115 (3), 715–753.

Alba, R., and Foner, N., 2016. Integration's Challenges and Opportunities in the Wealthy West. *Journal of Ethnic and Migration Studies*, 42 (1), 3–22.

Alba, R., and Nee, V., 2003. *Remaking the American Mainstream: Assimilation and Contemporary Immigration.* Cambridge, MA: Harvard University Press.

Alba, R., and Nee, V., 2005. *Remaking the American Mainstream: Assimilation and Contemporary Immigration.* Cambridge, MA: Harvard University Press.

Alba, R., and Silberman, R., 2002. Decolonization Immigration and the Social Origins of the Second Generation: The Case of North Africans in France. *International Migration Review*, 36 (4), 1169–1193.

Alba, R., and Waters, M. C., eds., 2011. *The Next Generation. Immigrant Youth in a Comparative Perspective.* New York: New York University Press.

Alba, R., Rumbaut, R. G., and Marotz, K., 2005. A Distorted Nation: Perceptions of Racial/Ethnic Group Sizes and Attitudes toward Immigrants and Other Minorities. *Social Forces*, 84 (2), 901–919.

Alesina, A. F., and Glaeser, E. L., 2004. *Fighting Poverty in the US and Europe.* New York: Oxford University Press.

Alesina, A., Harnoss, J., and Rapoport, H., 2016. Birthplace Diversity and Economic Prosperity. *Journal of Economic Growth*, 21 (2), 101–138.

Alesina, A., Michalopoulos, S., and Papaioannou, E., 2016. Ethnic Inequality. *Journal of Political Economy*, 124 (2), 428–488.

Alexander, J., 1992. Citizen and Enemy as Symbolic Classification: On the Polarizing Discourse of Civil Society. *In*: Lamont, M., and Fournier, M., eds., *Cultivating Differences:*

Symbolic Boundaries and the Making of Inequality. Chicago: Chicago University Press, 289–308.

Anderson, B., 2000. *Doing the Dirty Work? The Global Politics of Domestic Labour*. London: Zed Books.

Anderson, B., 2010. Migration, Immigration Controls and the Fashioning of Precarious Workers. *Work, Employment and Society*, 24 (2), 300–317.

Anderson, B., 2013. *Us and Them? The Dangerous Politics of Immigration Controls*. Oxford: Oxford University Press.

Anderson, B. R. O., 1983. *Imagined Communities: Reflections on the Origin and Spread of Nationalism*. London: Verso Books.

Aptekar, S., 2015. *The Road to Citizenship: What Naturalization Means for Immigrants and the United States*. New Brunswick: Rutgers University Press.

Aubry, A., Burzyński, M., and Docquier, F., 2016. The Welfare Impact of Global Migration in OECD Countries. *Journal of International Economics*, 101, 1–21.

Axelsson, R., and Westerlund, O., 1998. A Panel Study of Migration, Self-Selection and Household Real Income. *Journal of Population Economics*, 11 (1), 113–126.

Aydemir, A., 2011. Immigrant Selection and Short-Term Labor Market Outcomes by Visa Category. *Journal of Population Economics*, 24 (2), 451–475.

Aydemir, A., and Borjas, G. J., 2007. Cross-Country Variation in the Impact of International Migration: Canada, Mexico, and the United States. *Journal of the European Economic Association*, 5 (4), 663–708.

Bail, C. A., 2008. The Configuration of Symbolic Boundaries against Immigrants in Europe. *American Sociological Review*, 73, 37–59.

Banerjee, R., Kelly, P., Tungohan, E., Cleto, P., De Leon, C., Garcia, M., Luciano, M., Palmaria, C., and Sorio, C., 2018. From "Migrant" to "Citizen": Labor Market Integration of Former Live-In Caregivers in Canada. *Industrial and Labor Relations Review*, 71 (4), 908–936.

Banton, M., 1977. *The Idea of Race*. Boulder: Westview Press.

Banton, M., 1983. *Racial and Ethnic Competition*. Cambridge: Cambridge University Press.

Banton, M., 1998. *Racial Theories*. Cambridge: Cambridge University Press.

Banton, M., 2018. *What We Now Know about Race and Ethnicity.* New York: Berghahn Books.

Banulescu-Bogdan, N., and Papademetriou, D. G., 2016. *Understanding and Addressing Public Anxiety About Immigration.* Washington, DC: Migration Policy Institute.

Barone, G., and Mocetti, S., 2011. With a Little Help from Abroad: The Effect of Low-skilled Immigration on the Female Labour Supply. *Labour Economics*, 18 (5), 664–675.

Barron, P., Bory, A., Chauvin, S., Jounin, N., and Tourette, L., 2014. Derrière le sans-papiers, le travailleur? Genèse et usages de la catégorie de "travailleurs sans papiers" en France. *Genèses*, 94 (1), 114–139.

Barron, P., Bory, A., Tourette, L., Chauvin, S., and Jounin, N., 2011. *On bosse ici, on reste ici! La grève des sans-papiers : Une aventure inédite.* Paris: La Découverte.

Barth, F., 1969. *Ethnic Groups and Boundaries: The Social Organization of Culture Differences.* London: Allen & Unwin.

Basch, L., Glick Schiller, N., and Szanton Blanc, C., 1994. *Nations Unbound: Transnational Projects, Postcolonial Predicaments and Deterritorialized Nation-States.* Langhorne: Gordon & Breach.

Bashi, V., 2004. Globalized Anti-Blackness: Transnationalizing Western Immigration Law, Policy, and Practice. *Ethnic & Racial Studies*, 27 (4), 584–606.

Bauböck, R., 1994. *Transnational Citizenship: Membership and Rights in International Migration.* Aldershot: Edward Elgar Publishing.

Bauböck, R., 1998. Sharing History and Future? *Constellations*, 4 (3), 320–345.

Bauböck, R., 2010. Cold Constellations and Hot Identities: Political Theory Questions about Transnationalism and Diaspora. *In*: Baubök, R., and Faist, T., eds., *Diaspora and Transnationalism.* Amsterdam: Amsterdam University Press, 296–321.

Beaman, J., 2015. Boundaries of Frenchness: Cultural Citizenship and France's Middle-Class North African Second Generation. *Identities*, 22 (1), 36–52.

Beaman, J., 2016. Citizenship as Cultural: Towards a Theory of Cultural Citizenship. *Sociology Compass*, 10 (10), 849–857.

Bean, F. D., and Bell-Rose, S., eds., 1999. *Immigration and Opportunity: Race, Ethnicity, and Employment in the United States.* New York: Russell Sage Foundation.

Beauchemin, C., and Safi, M., 2019. Migrants' Connections Within and Beyond Borders: Insights from the Comparison of Three Categories of Migrants in France. *Ethnic and Racial Studies*. Available from: https://doi.org/10.1080/01419870.2 019.1572906.

Beauchemin, C., Hamel, C., and Simon, P., eds., 2015. *Trajectoires et origines: Enquête sur la diversité des populations en France*. Paris: Institut National d'Études Démographiques.

Becker, G., 1964. *Human Capital. A Theoretical and Empirical Analysis, with Special Reference to Education*. Chicago: University Press of Chicago

Beerli, A., and Peri, G., 2018. The Labor Market Effects of Opening the Border: Evidence from Switzerland. *National Bureau of Economic Research*, Working Paper 21319.

Beine, M., Docquier, F., and Rapoport, H., 2008. Brain Drain and Human Capital Formation in Developing Countries: Winners and Losers. *Economic Journal*, 118 (528), 631–652.

Bell, M., and Charles-Edward, E., 2013. *Cross-National Comparisons of Internal Migration: An Update of Global Patterns and Trends*. New York: United Nations.

Belot, M. V. K., and Hatton, T. J., 2012. Immigrant Selection in the OECD. *Scandinavian Journal of Economics*, 114 (4), 1105–1128.

Berezin, M., and Schain, M., eds., 2004. *Europe without Borders: Remapping Territory, Citizenship, and Identity in a Transnational Age*. Baltimore: Johns Hopkins University Press.

Berger, J., and Webster, M., 2006. Expectations, Status, and Behavior. *In*: Burke, P., ed., *Contemporary Social Psychological Theories*. Stanford: Stanford University Press, 268–300.

Berger, S., 2009. (Un)Worthy: Latina Battered Immigrants under VAWA and the Construction of Neoliberal Subjects. *Citizenship Studies*, 13 (3), 201–217.

Berry, J. W., 2001. A Psychology of Immigration. *Journal of Social Issues*, 57 (3), 615–631.

Berry, J. W., Kim, U., Minde, T., and Mok, D., 1987. Comparative Studies of Acculturative Stress. *International Migration Review*, 21 (3), 491–511.

Berry, M., Garcia-Blanco, I., and Moore, K., 2016. *Press Coverage of the Refugee and Migrant Crisis in the EU: A Content Analysis of Five European Countries*. Office of the United Nations High Commissioner for Refugees.

Bertrand, M., Chugh, D., and Mullainathan, S., 2005. Implicit Discrimination. *American Economic Review*, 95 (2), 94–98.

Blau, F. D., and Kahn, L. M., 2015. Immigration and the Distribution of Incomes. *In*: Chiswick, B. R., and Miller, P. W., eds., *Handbook of the Economics of International Migration*. Amsterdam: North-Holland, 793–843.

Blau, P. M., 1977. *Inequality and Heterogeneity: A Primitive Theory of Social Structure*. New York: Free Press.

Blauner, R., 1972. *Racial Oppression in America*. New York: Harper & Row.

Bloemraad, I., Korteweg, A., and Yurdakul, G., 2008. Citizenship and Immigration: Multiculturalism, Assimilation, and Challenges to the Nation-State. *Annual Review of Sociology*, 34 (1), 153–179.

Blumer, H., 1958. Race Prejudice as a Sense of Group Position. *Pacific Sociological Review*, 1 (1), 3–7.

Boneva, B. S., and Frieze, I. H., 2001. Toward a Concept of a Migrant Personality. *Journal of Social Issues*, 57 (3), 477–491.

Bonilla-Silva, E., 1999. The Essential Social Fact of Race. *American Sociological Review*, 64 (6), 899–906.

Bonilla-Silva, E., 2004. From Bi-racial to Tri-racial: Towards a New System of Racial Stratification in the USA. *Ethnic and Racial Studies*, 27 (6), 931–950.

Boris, E., and Janssens, A., eds., 1999. *Complicating Categories: Gender, Class, Race and Ethnicity*. Cambridge: Cambridge University Press.

Borjas, G. J., 1987. Immigrants, Minorities, and Labor Market Competition. *Industrial and Labor Relations Review*, 40 (3), 382–392.

Borjas, G. J., 1989. Economic Theory and International Migration. *International Migration Review*, 23 (3), 457–485.

Borjas, G. J., 1994. The Economics of Immigration. *Journal of Economic Literature*, 32 (4), 1667–1717.

Borjas, G. J., 1999. The Economic Analysis of Immigration. *In*: Ashenfelter, O., and Card, D., eds., *Handbook of Labor Economics*. Amsterdam: Elsevier, 1697–1760.

Borjas, G. J., 2003. The Labor Demand Curve is Downward Sloping: Reexamining the Impact of Immigration on the Labor Market. *Quarterly Journal of Economics*, 118 (4), 1335–1374.

Borjas, G. J., 2014. *Immigration Economis*. Cambridge MA: Harvard University Press.

Borjas, G. J., Bronars, S. G., and Trejo, S. J., 1992. Self-Selection and Internal Migration in the United States. *Journal of Urban Economics*, 32 (2), 159–185.

Bourdieu, P., 1982. Ce que parler veut dire : L'économie des échanges linguistiques. *L'Homme et la Société*, 65–66, 197–198.

Bourdieu, P., 1984. *Distinction: A Social Critique of the Judgement of Taste*. Cambridge, MA: Harvard University Press.

Bourdieu, P., 1986. The Forms of Capital. *In*: Richardson, J. G., ed., *Handbook of Theory and Research for the Sociology of Education*. New York: Greenwood Publishing Group, 241–258.

Bove, V., and Elia, L., 2017. Migration, Diversity, and Economic Growth. *World Development*, 89 (C), 227–239.

Bowker, G. C., and Star, S. L., 2000. *Sorting Things Out: Classification and Its Consequences*. Cambridge, MA: MIT Press.

Bowles, S., Smith, E. A., and Mulder, M. B., 2010. The Emergence and Persistence of Inequality in Premodern Societies: Introduction to the Special Section. *Current Anthropology*, 51 (1), 7–17.

Boyle, P., Cooke, T. J., Halfacree, K., and Smith, D., 2001. A Cross-National Comparison of the Impact of Family Migration on Women's Employment Status. *Demography*, 38 (2), 201–213.

Brady, D., and Finnigan, R., 2013. Does Immigration Undermine Public Support for Social Policy? *American Sociological Review*, 79 (1), 17–42.

Bratsberg, B., Ragan, J., and Nasir, Z., 2002. The Effect of Naturalization on Wage Growth: A Panel Study of Young Male Immigrants. *Journal of Labor Economics*, 20 (3), 568–597.

Brown, C., Eichengreen, B. J., and Reich, M., eds., 2009. *Labor in the Era of Globalization*. New York: Cambridge University Press.

Brown, H. E., 2011. Refugees, Rights, and Race: How Legal Status Shapes Liberian Immigrants' Relationship with the State. *Social Problems*, 58 (1), 144–163.

Brown, H. E., 2013. Race, Legality, and the Social Policy Consequences of Anti-Immigration Mobilization. *American Sociological Review*, 78 (2), 290–314.

Brubaker, R., 1992. *Citizenship and Nationhood in France and Germany*. Cambridge, MA: Harvard University Press.

Brubaker, R., 1998. Migrations of Ethnic Unmixing in the "New Europe." *International Migration Review*, 32 (4), 1047–1065.

Brubaker, R., 2001. The Return of Assimilation? Changing Perspectives on Immigration and its Sequels in France, Germany, and the United States. *Ethnic and Racial Studies*, 24 (4), 531–548.

Brubaker, R., 2002. Ethnicity without Groups. *European Journal of Sociology*, 43 (02), 163–189.

Brubaker, R., 2009. Ethnicity, Race, and Nationalism. *Annual Review of Sociology*, 35 (1), 21–42.

Brubaker, R., 2010. Migration, Membership, and the Modern Nation-State: Internal and External Dimensions of the Politics of Belonging. *Journal of Interdisciplinary History*, 41 (1), 61–78.

Brubaker, R., 2015. *Grounds for Difference*. Cambridge, MA: Harvard University Press.

Brubaker, R., and Cooper, F., 2000. Beyond "Identity." *Theory and Society*, 29 (1), 1–47.

Brubaker, R., and Laitin, D. D., 1998. Ethnic and Nationalist Violence. *Annual Review of Sociology*, 24, 423–452.

Brubaker, R., Loveman, M., and Stamatov, P., 2004. Ethnicity as Cognition. *Theory and Society*, 33 (1), 31–64.

Bullock, H., 2008. Justifying Inequality: A Social Psychological Analysis of Beliefs about Poverty and the Poor. *In*: Lin, A. C., and Harris, D. R., eds., *The Colors of Poverty: Why Racial and Ethnic Disparities Persist*. New York: Russell Sage Foundation.

Bunzl, M., 2005. Between Anti-Semitism and Islamophobia: Some Thoughts on the New Europe. *American Ethnologist*, 32 (4), 499–508.

Calavita, K., 1992. *Inside the State: The Bracero Program, Immigration, and the INS*. Abingdon: Routledge.

Calavita, K., 2005. *Immigrants at the Margin: Law, Race, and Exclusion in Southern Europe*. Cambridge: Cambridge University Press.

Calavita, K., 2007. Immigration Law, Race, and Identity. *Annual Review of Law and Social Science*, 3 (1), 1–20.

Capetillo-Ponce, J., 2008. Framing the Debate on Taxes and Undocumented Workers: A Critical Review of Texts Supporting Pro-Enforcement Policies and Practices. *In*: Brotherton, D. C., and Kretsedemas, P., eds., *Keeping Out the Other: A Critical Introduction to Immigration Enforcement Today*. New York: Columbia University Press.

Card, D., 1990. The Impact of the Mariel Boatlift on the Miami Labor Market. *Industrial and Labor Relations Review*, 43 (2), 245–257.

Card, D., 2009. Immigration and Inequality. *American Economic Review*, 99 (2), 1–21.

Card, D., and Peri, G., 2016. Immigration Economics by George J. Borjas: A Review Essay, *Journal of Economic Literature*, 54 (4), 1333–1349.

Carling, J., 2007. Migration Control and Migrant Fatalities at the Spanish–African Borders. *International Migration Review*, 41 (2), 316–343.

Carling, J., and Collins, F., 2018. Aspiration, Desire and Drivers of Migration. *Journal of Ethnic and Migration Studies*, 44 (6), 909–926.

Caron, L., 2018. Whose Integration Do We Measure? Immigrants' Remigration and Labour Market Integration in France. *Population*, 73 (3), 481–518.

Carrasquillo, O., Carrasquillo, A. I., and Shea, S., 2000. Health Insurance Coverage of Immigrants Living in the United States: Differences by Citizenship Status and Country of Origin. *American Journal of Public Health*, 90 (6), 917–923.

Castañeda, H., Holmes, S. M., Madrigal, D. S., Young, M.-E. D., Beyeler, N., and Quesada, J., 2015. Immigration as a Social Determinant of Health. *Annual Review of Public Health*, 36 (1), 375–392.

Castles, S., 2005. Nation and Empire: Hierarchies of Citizenship in the New Global Order. *International Politics*, 42 (2), 203–224.

Castles, S., 2011. Migration, Crisis, and the Global Labour Market. *Globalizations*, 8 (3), 311–324.

Castles, S., and Kosack, G., 1973. *Immigrant Workers and Class Structure in Western Europe*. London: Oxford University Press.

Cerna, L., 2008. Towards an EU Blue Card? The Delegation of National High Skilled Immigration Policies to the EU Level.

ESRC Centre on Migration, Policy and Society, Working Paper 65.

Cerrutti, M., and Massey, D. S., 2001. On the Auspices of Female Migration from Mexico to the United States. Demography, 38 (2), 187–200.

Césaire, A., 1987. Discours sur la Négritude. Miami: Florida International University.

Charles, M., 2008. Culture and Inequality: Identity, Ideology, and Difference in "Postascriptive Society." Annals of the American Academy of Political and Social Science, 619 (1), 41–58.

Chauvin, S., and Garcés-Mascareñas, B., 2012. Beyond Informal Citizenship: The New Moral Economy of Migrant Illegality. International Political Sociology, 6 (3), 241–259.

Chauvin, S., and Garcés-Mascareñas, B., 2014. Becoming Less Illegal: Deservingness Frames and Undocumented Migrant Incorporation. Sociology Compass, 8 (4), 422–432.

Chauvin, S., Garcés-Mascareñas, B., and Kraler, A., 2013. Working for Legality: Employment and Migrant Regularization in Europe. International Migration, 51 (6), 118–131.

Chavez, L. R., 2008. The Latino Threat: Constructing Immigrants, Citizens, and the Nation. Stanford: Stanford University Press.

Chiswick, B. R. 1978. The Effect of Americanization on the Earnings of Foreign-Born Men. Journal of Political Economy, 86 (5), 897–921.

Choldin, H. M., 1986. Statistics and Politics: The "Hispanic Issue" in the 1980 Census. Demography, 23 (3), 403–418.

Chwe, M. S.-Y., 2001. Rational Ritual: Culture, Coordination and Common Knowledge. Princeton: Princeton University Press.

Clark, X., Hatton, T. J., and Williamson, J. G., 2007. Explaining US Immigration, 1971–1998. Review of Economics and Statistics, 89 (2), 359–373.

Clemens, M. A., 2010. The Roots of Global Wage Gaps: Evidence from Randomized Processing of US Visas. Center for Global Development, Working Paper 212.

Clemens, M. A., 2011. Economics and Emigration: Trillion-Dollar Bills on the Sidewalk? Journal of Economic Perspectives, 25 (3), 83–106.

Clemens, M. A., 2017. Violence, Development, and Migration

Waves: Evidence from Central American Child Migrant Apprehensions. *Center for Global Development*, Working Paper 459.

Cohen, R., 2006. *Migration and its Enemies: Global Capital, Migrant Labour and the Nation-State*. London: Routledge.

Collins, R., 1999. *Macrohistory: Essays in Sociology of the Long Run*. Stanford: Stanford University Press.

Collins, R., 2001. Ethnic Change in Macro-Historical Perspective. *In*: Anderson, E., and Massey, D. S., eds., *Problem of the Century. Racial Stratification in the United States*. New York: Russell Sage Foundation, 13–46.

Collins, R., 2005. *Interaction Ritual Chains*. Princeton: Princeton University Press.

Collyer, M., and De Haas, H., 2012. Developing Dynamic Categorisations of Transit Migration. *Population, Space and Place*, 18 (4), 468–481.

Connell, R. W., 1997. Why Is Classical Theory Classical? *American Journal of Sociology*, 102 (6), 1511–1557.

Cook-Martín, D., and FitzGerald, D., 2010. Liberalism and the Limits of Inclusion: Race and Immigration Law in the Americas 1850–2000. *Journal of Interdisciplinary History*, 41 (1), 7–26.

Corluy, V., Marx, I., and Verbist, G., 2011. Employment Chances and Changes of Immigrants in Belgium: The Impact of Citizenship. *International Journal of Comparative Sociology*, 52 (4), 350–368.

Cornell, S., and Hartmann, D., 1998. *Ethnicity and Race: Making Identities in a Changing World*. Thousand Oaks: Pine Forge Press.

Cornell, S., and Hartmann, D., 2004. Conceptual Confusions and Divides: Race, Ethnicity, and the Study of Immigration. *In*: Foner, N., and Frederickson, G., eds., *Not Just Black and White: Historical and Contemporary Perspectives on Immigration, Race, and Ethnicity in the United States*. New York: Russell Sage Foundation, 23–41.

Cortés, P., and Tessada, J., 2011. Low-Skilled Immigration and the Labor Supply of Highly Skilled Women. *American Economic Journal: Applied Economics*, 3 (3), 88–123.

Cosquer, C., 2018. Expat' à Abu Dhabi: Blanchité et construction du groupe national chez les migrant. Doctoral thesis. Sciences Po Paris.

Coutin, S. B., 1998. From Refugees to Immigrants: The

Legalization Strategies of Salvadoran Immigrants and Activists. *International Migration Review*, 32 (4), 901–925.

Coutin, S. B., 2000. *Legalizing Moves: Salvadoran Immigrants' Struggle for US Residency.* Ann Arbor: University of Michigan Press.

Coutin, S. B., 2011. The Rights of Noncitizens in the United States. *Annual Review of Law and Social Science*, 7 (1), 289–308.

Couto, M.-P., 2013. L'Intégration socio-économique des pieds-noirs en France métropolitaine: Le lien de citoyenneté à l'épreuve. *Revue Européenne des Migrations Internationales*, 29 (3), 93–119.

Cox, O. C., 1948. *Caste, Class, and Race: A Study in Social Dynamics.* New York: Monthly Review Press.

Crawley, H., and Skleparis, D., 2018. Refugees, Migrants, Neither, Both: Categorical Fetishism and the Politics of Bounding in Europe's "Migration Crisis." *Journal of Ethnic and Migration Studies*, 44 (1), 48–64.

Crenshaw, K., 1991. Mapping the Margins: Intersectionality, Identity Politics, and Violence against Women of Color. *Stanford Law Review*, 43 (6), 1241–1299.

Curran, S. R., and Rivero-Fuentes, E., 2003. Engendering Migrant Networks: The Case of Mexican Migration. *Demography*, 40 (2), 289–307.

Czaika, M., and De Haas, H., 2014. The Globalization of Migration: Has the World Become More Migratory? *International Migration Review*, 48 (2), 283–323.

Dacosta, K. M., 2007. *Making Multiracials: State, Family and Market in the Redrawing of the Color Line.* Stanford: Stanford University Press.

Dahl, R. A., 1989. *Democracy and Its Critics.* New Haven: Yale University Press.

D'Amuri, F., and Peri, G., 2014. Immigration, Jobs, and Employment Protection: Evidence from Europe Before and During the Great Recession. *Journal of the European Economic Association*, 12 (2), 432–464.

Davis, K., and Moore, W. E., 1945. Some Principles of Stratification. *American Sociological Review*, 10 (2), 242–249.

De Genova, N. P., 2002. Migrant "Illegality" and Deportability in Everyday Life. *Annual Review of Anthropology*, 31 (1), 419–447.

De Wenden, C. W., Schmoll, C., and Thiollet, H., 2015. *Migrations en Méditerranée*. Paris: Centre National de la Recherche Scientifique.

Deaton, A., 2015. *The Great Escape: Health, Wealth, and the Origins of Inequality*. Princeton: Princeton University Press.

Deaux, K., 1993. Reconstructing Social Identity. *Personality and Social Psychology Bulletin*, 19 (1), 4–12.

DeFreitas, G., 1991. *Inequality at Work: Hispanics in the US Labor Force*. New York: Oxford University Press.

Desmet, K., Ortuño-Ortín, I., and Wacziarg, R., 2017. Culture, Ethnicity, and Diversity. *American Economic Review*, 107 (9), 2479–2513.

Desmet, K., Ortuño-Ortín, I., and Weber, S., 2009. Linguistic Diversity and Redistribution. *Journal of the European Economic Association*, 7 (6), 1291–1318.

Devine, P. G., 2001. Implicit Prejudice and Stereotyping: How Automatic Are They? Introduction to the Special Section. *Journal of Personality and Social Psychology*, 81 (5), 757–759.

Diaz, G., and Kuhner, G., 2009. *Women Migrants in Detention in Mexico: Conditions and Due Process*. Washington, DC: Migration Policy Institute.

DiMaggio, P., 1997. Culture and Cognition. *Annual Review of Sociology*, 23, 263–287.

DiTomaso, N., Post, C., and Parks-Yancy, R., 2007. Workforce Diversity and Inequality: Power, Status, and Numbers. *Annual Review of Sociology*, 33 (1), 473–501.

Docquier, F., and Rapoport, H., 2012. Globalization, Brain Drain, and Development. *Journal of Economic Literature*, 50 (3), 681–730.

Doeringer, P., and Piore, M. J., 1971. *Internal Labor Markets and Manpower Analysis*. Lexington: D. C. Heath and Company.

Donato, K. M., and Armenta, A., 2011. What We Know About Unauthorized Migration. *Annual Review of Sociology*, 37 (1), 529–543.

Dreby, J., 2012. The Burden of Deportation on Children in Mexican Immigrant Families. *Journal of Marriage and Family*, 74 (4), 829–845.

Dreby, J., 2015. *Everyday Illegal: When Policies Undermine Immigrant Families*. Berkeley: University of California Press.

Duleep, H. O., 2015. The Adjustment of Immigrants in the Labor Market. *In*: Chiswick, B. R., and Miller, P. W., eds.,

Handbook of the Economics of International Migration. Amsterdam: North-Holland, 105–182.

Dustmann, C., and Preston, I., 2007. Racial and Economic Factors in Attitudes to Immigration. *BE Journal of Economic Analysis and Policy*, 7 (1), Article 62.

Dustmann, C., Frattini, T., and Preston, I. P., 2013. The Effect of Immigration along the Distribution of Wages. *Review of Economic Studies*, 80 (1), 145–173.

Dustmann, C., Hatton, T., and Preston, I., 2005. The Labour Market Effects of Immigration. *Economic Journal*, 115 (507), F297–F299.

Dustmann, C., Ludsteck, J., and Schönberg, U., 2009. Revisiting the German Wage Structure. *Quarterly Journal of Economics*, 124 (2), 843–881.

Dustmann, C., Schönberg, U., and Stuhler, J., 2016. The Impact of Immigration: Why Do Studies Reach Such Different Results? *Journal of Economic Perspectives*, 30 (4), 31–56.

Eckstein, S., 2002. On Deconstructing and Reconstructing the Meaning of Immigrant Generations. *In*: Levitt, P., and Waters, M. C., eds., *The Changing Face of Home: The Transnational Lives of the Second Generation.* New York: Russell Sage Foundation, 211–215.

Eckstein, S., and Peri, G., eds., 2018. New Immigrant Labour Niches. *Russell Sage Foundation Journal of the Social Sciences*, 4 (1).

Elrick, J., and Lightman, N., 2016. Sorting or Shaping? The Gendered Economic Outcomes of Immigration Policy in Canada. *International Migration Review*, 50 (2), 352–384.

Emirbayer, M., and Desmond, M., 2015. *The Racial Order.* Chicago: University of Chicago Press.

Escafré-Dublet, A., Kesztenbaum, L., and Simon, P., 2018. La Greffe coloniale en métropole. *Sociétés contemporaines*, 110 (2), 35–59.

Eschbach, K., Hagan, J., Rodriguez, N., Hernandez-Leon, R., and Bailey, S., 1999. Death at the Border. *International Migration Review*, 33 (2), 430–454.

Espiritu, Y. L., 1992. *Asian American Panethnicity: Bridging Institutions and Identities.* Philadelphia: Temple University Press.

EU, 2013. *Using EU Indicators of Immigrant Integration. Final*

Report for Directorate-General for Home Affairs. European Commission.

EU, 2018. *EU Budget for the Future: Migration and Border Management*. European Commission.

Faist, T., 2000. *The Volume and Dynamics of International Migration and Transnational Spaces*. New York: Oxford University Press.

Faist, T., 2016. Cross-Border Migration and Social Inequalities. *Annual Review of Sociology*, 42 (1), 323–346.

Faist, T., and Kivisto, P., eds., 2007. *Dual Citizenship in Global Perspective: From Unitary to Multiple Citizenship*. New York: Palgrave Macmillan.

Farris, S. R., 2012. Femonationalism and the "Regular" Army of Labor Called Migrant Women. *History of the Present*, 2 (2), 184–199.

Fassin, D., 2001. The Biopolitics of Otherness: Undocumented Foreigners and Racial Discrimination in French Public Debate. *Anthropology Today*, 17 (1), 3–7.

Fassin, D., 2005. Compassion and Repression: The Moral Economy of Immigration Policies in France. *Cultural Anthropology*, 20 (3), 362–387.

Fassin, D., and D'halluin, E., 2005. The Truth from the Body: Medical Certificates as Ultimate Evidence for Asylum Seekers. *American Anthropologist*, 107 (4), 597–608.

Fassin, D., Morice, A., and Quiminal, C., 1997. *Les Lois de l'inhospitalité. Les politiques de l'immigration à l'épreuve des sans-papiers*. Paris: La Découverte.

Favell, A., 2001. Integration Policy and Integration Research in Europe: A Review and Critique. *In*: Aleinikoff, A., and Klusmeyer, D., eds., *Citizenship Today: Global Perspectives and Practices*. Washington, DC: Brookings Institute, 349–399.

Favell, A., 2008. The New Face of East–West Migration in Europe. *Journal of Ethnic and Migration Studies*, 34 (5), 701–716.

Felbermayr, G., Grossmann, V., and Kohler, W., 2015. Migration, International Trade, and Capital Formation: Cause or Effect? *In*: Chiswick, B. R., and Miller, P. W., eds., *Handbook of the Economics of International Migration*. Amsterdam: North-Holland, 913–1025.

Feliciano, C., 2009. Education and Ethnic Identity Formation among Children of Latin American and Caribbean Immigrants. *Sociological Perspectives*, 52 (2), 135–158.

Feliciano, C., 2016. Shades of Race: How Phenotype and Observer Characteristics Shape Racial Classification. *American Behavioral Scientist*, 60 (4), 390–419.

Feliciano, C., and Rumbaut, R. G., 2018. Varieties of Ethnic Self-Identities: Children of Immigrants in Middle Adulthood. *Russell Sage Foundation Journal of the Social Sciences*, 4 (5), 26–46.

Fisher, M. H., 2014. *Migration: A World History*. Oxford: Oxford University Press.

Fiske, S. T., 1998. Stereotyping, Prejudice, and Discrimination. *In*: Gilbert, D. T., Fiske, S. T., and Lindzey, G., eds., *Handbook of Social Psychology*. New York: McGraw Hill, 554–594.

Fiske, S. T., and Taylor, S. E., 1991. *Social Cognition*. New York: McGraw Hill.

Fiske, S. T., Cuddy, A. J. C., Glick, P., and Xu, J., 2002. A Model of (Often Mixed) Stereotype Content: Competence and Warmth Respectively Follow from Perceived Status and Competition. *Journal of Personality and Social Psychology*, 82 (6), 878–902.

FitzGerald, D. S., 2006. Inside the Sending State: The Politics of Mexican Emigration Control. *International Migration Review*, 40 (2), 259–293.

FitzGerald, D. S., 2017. The History of Racialized Citizenship. *In*: Shachar, A., Bauböck, R., Bloemraad, I., and Vink, M., eds., *The Oxford Handbook of Citizenship*. Oxford Handbooks Online.

FitzGerald, D. S., and Arar, R., 2018. The Sociology of Refugee Migration. *Annual Review of Sociology*, 44 (1), 387–406.

Fitzgerald, J., Leblang, D., and Teets, J. C., 2014. Defying the Law of Gravity: The Political Economy of International Migration. *World Politics*, 66 (03), 406–445.

Fix, M., Hallock, J., and Soto, A. G. R., 2018. *In Search of Safety, Growing Numbers of Women Flee Central America*. Washington, DC: Migration Policy Institute.

Foner, N., 2005. *In a New Land: A Comparative View of Immigration*. New York: New York University Press.

Foner, N., 2015. Is Islam in Western Europe Like Race in the United States? *Sociological Forum*, 30 (4), 885–899.

Foner, N., Deaux, K., and Donato, K. M., 2018. Introduction: Immigration and Changing Identities. *Russell Sage Foundation Journal of the Social Sciences*, 4 (5), 1–25.

Fougère, D., and Safi, M., 2009. Naturalization and Employment of Immigrants in France (1968–1999). *International Journal of Manpower*, 30 (1/2), 83–96.

Fouron, G. E., and Glick Schiller, N., 2002. The Generation of Identity: Redefining the Second Generation within a Transnational Social Field. *In*: Levitt, P., and Waters, M. C., eds., *The Changing Face of Home: The Transnational Lives of the Second Generation*. New York: Russell Sage Foundation, 168–210.

Fox, C., 2012. *Three Worlds of Relief: Race, Immigration, and the American Welfare State from the Progressive Era to the New Deal*. Princeton: Princeton University Press.

Fox, C., and Bloemraad, I., 2015. Beyond "White by Law": Explaining the Gulf in Citizenship Acquisition between Mexican and European Immigrants, 1930. *Social Forces*, 94 (1), 181–207.

Fox, C., and Guglielmo, T. A., 2012. Defining America's Racial Boundaries: Blacks, Mexicans, and European Immigrants, 1890–1945. *American Journal of Sociology*, 118 (2), 327–379.

Fox, J. E., 2013. The Uses of Racism: Whitewashing New Europeans in the UK. *Ethnic and Racial Studies*, 36 (11), 1871–1889.

Fox, J. E., Moroşanu, L., and Szilassy, E., 2012. The Racialization of the New European Migration to the UK. *Sociology*, 46 (4), 680–695.

Frank, R., Akresh, I. R., and Lu, B., 2010. Latino Immigrants and the US Racial Order: How and Where Do They Fit In? *American Sociological Review*, 75 (3), 378–401.

Frankenberg, R., 1993. *White Women, Race Matters: The Social Construction of Whiteness*. Minneapolis: University of Minnesota Press.

Fredrickson, G. M., 2002. *Racism: A Short History*. Princeton: Princeton University Press.

Freeman, G., 1995. Modes of Immigration Politics in Liberal Democratic States. *International Migration Review*, 29 (4), 881–902.

Galli, C., 2017. A Rite of Reverse Passage: The Construction of Youth Migration in the US Asylum Process. *Ethnic and Racial Studies*, 41 (9), 1651–1671.

Galster, G., and Sharkey, P., 2017. Spatial Foundations of Inequality: A Conceptual Model and Empirical Overview.

Russell Sage Foundation Journal of the Social Sciences, 3 (2), 1–33.

Gans, H. J., 1997. Toward a Reconciliation of Assimilation and Pluralism: The Interplay of Acculturation and Ethnic Retention. *International Migration Review*, 31 (4), 875–892.

Gans, H. J., 1999. *The Possibility of a New Racial Hierarchy in the Twenty-First Century United States.* Chicago: University of Chicago Press.

Garcés-Mascareñas, B., and Penninx, R., eds., 2015. *Integration Processes and Policies in Europe: Contexts, Levels, and Actors.* New York: Springer.

Gathmann, C., and Keller, N., 2014. Returns to Citizenship? Evidence from Germany's Recent Immigration Reforms. *CESifo*, Working Paper 4738.

Glazer, N., 1993. Is Assimilation Dead? *Annals of the American Academy of Political and Social Science*, 530, 122–136.

Glick Schiller, N., Basch, L., and Blanc-Szanton, C., 1992. *Toward a Transnational Perspective on Migration.* New York: New York Academy of Sciences.

Golash-Boza, T., 2006. Dropping the Hyphen? Becoming Latino(a)-American through Racialized Assimilation. *Social Forces*, 85 (1), 27–55.

Golash-Boza, T., and Darity, W., 2008. Latino Racial Choices: The Effects of Skin Colour and Discrimination on Latinos' and Latinas' Racial Self-identifications. *Ethnic and Racial Studies*, 31 (5), 899–934.

Goldberg, D. T., 1993. *Racist Culture: Philosophy and the Politics of Meaning.* Oxford: Blackwell.

Goldberg, D. T., 2002. *The Racial State.* Malden: Blackwell.

Goldberg, D. T., 2009. *The Threat of Race: Reflections on Racial Neoliberalism.* Oxford: Wiley-Blackwell.

Gonzales, R. G., 2011. Learning to Be Illegal: Undocumented Youth and Shifting Legal Contexts in the Transition to Adulthood. *American Sociological Review*, 76 (4), 602–619.

Gordon, M. M., 1964. *Assimilation in American life: The Role of Race, Religion, and National Origins.* New York: Oxford University Press.

Gotanda, N., 2011. The Racialization of Islam in American Law. *Annals of the American Academy of Political and Social Science*, 637 (1), 184–195.

Green, N. L., 2002. *Repenser les migrations*. Paris: Presses Universitaires de France.

Green, N. L., and Waldinger, R. D., 2016. *A Century of Transnationalism: Immigrants and Their Homeland Connections*. Urbana: University of Illinois Press.

Greenman, E., and Hall, M., 2013. Legal Status and Educational Transitions for Mexican and Central American Immigrant Youth. *Social Forces*, 91 (4), 1475–1498.

Greenwald, A. G., and Banaji, M. R., 1995. Implicit Social Cognition: Attitudes, Self-Esteem, and Stereotypes. *Psychological Review*, 102 (1), 4–27.

Greenwald, A. G., and Krieger, L. H., 2006. Implicit Bias: Scientific Foundations. *California Law Review*, 94 (4), 945–967.

Grogger, J., and Hanson, G. H., 2011. Income Maximization and the Selection and Sorting of International Migrants. *Journal of Development Economics*, 95 (1), 42–57.

Grusky, D. B., and Ku, M. C., 2008. Gloom, Doom, and Inequality. *In*: Grusky, D. B., Ku, M. C., and Szelenyi, S., eds., *Social Stratification: Class, Race, and Gender in Sociological Perspective*. Boulder: Westview Press, 2–28.

Grusky, D. B., Ku, M. C., and Szelenyi, S., eds., 2008. *Social Stratification: Class, Race, and Gender in Sociological Perspective*. Boulder: Westview Press.

Guillaumin, C., 1985. Sur la notion de minorité. *L'Homme et la Société*, 101–109.

Guiraudon, V., 2003. The Constitution of a European Immigration Policy Domain: A Political Sociology Approach. *Journal of European Public Policy*, 10 (2), 263–282.

Guiraudon, V., and Joppke, C., eds., 2001. *Controlling a New Migration*. London: Routledge.

Haddad, M., 2018. Migration from French Overseas Departments to Metropolitan France: What We Can Learn About a State Policy from the Censuses, 1962–1999. *Population*, 73 (2), 181–216.

Hainmueller, J., and Hopkins, D. J., 2014. Public Attitudes Toward Immigration. *Annual Review of Political Science*, 17 (1), 225–249.

Hainmueller, J., Hangartner, D., and Pietrantuono, G., 2015. Naturalization Fosters the Long-term Political Integration of Immigrants. *Proceedings of the National Academy of Sciences*, 112 (41), 12651–12656.

Hainmueller, J., Lawrence, D., Martén, L., Black, B., Figueroa, L., Hotard, M., Jiménez, T. R., Mendoza, F., Rodriguez, M. I., Swartz, J. J., and Laitin, D. D., 2017. Protecting Unauthorized Immigrant Mothers Improves Their Children's Mental Health. *Science*, 357 (6355), 1041–1044.

Hall, M., and Greenman, E., 2015. The Occupational Cost of Being Illegal in the United States: Legal Status, Job Hazards, and Compensating Differentials. *International Migration Review*, 49 (2), 406–442.

Hall, M., Greenman, E., and Farkas, G., 2010. Legal Status and Wage Disparities for Mexican Immigrants. *Social Forces*, 89 (2), 491–513.

Hall, S., 1994. Culture Identity and Diaspora. *In*: Williams, P., and Chrisman, L., eds., *Colonial Discourse and Post-Colonial Theory: A Reader*. New York: Harvester-Wheatsheaf, 392–403.

Haller, W., and Landolt, P., 2005. The Transnational Dimensions of Identity Formation: Adult Children of Immigrants in Miami. *Ethnic & Racial Studies*, 28 (6), 1182–1214.

Hanke, L., 1970. *Aristotle and the American Indians: A Study in Race Prejudice in the Modern World*. Bloomington: Indiana University Press.

Hansen, R., 2000. *Citizenship and Immigration in Postwar Britain*. New York: Oxford University Press.

Hanson, G. H., and Slaughter, M. J., 2016. High-Skilled Immigration and the Rise of STEM Occupations in US Employment. *National Bureau of Economic Research*, Working Paper 22623.

Harris, L. T., and Fiske, S. T., 2006. Dehumanizing the Lowest of the Low. *Psychological Science*, 17 (10), 847–853.

Harrison, J. L., and Lloyd, S. E., 2013. New Jobs, New Workers, and New Inequalities: Explaining Employers' Roles in Occupational Segregation by Nativity and Race. *Social Problems*, 60 (3), 281–301.

Hatton, T., 2014. The Economics of International Migration: A Short History of the Debate. *Labour Economics*, 30 (C), 43–50.

Hatton, T., 2016. Refugees, Asylum Seekers and Policy in OECD Countries. *American Economic Review*, 106, 441–445.

Hatton, T. J., and Williamson, J. G., 1998. *The Age of Mass Migration: Causes and Economic Impact*. New York: Oxford University Press.

Heath, A., and Cheung, S. Y., eds., 2007. *Unequal Chances: Ethnic Minorities in Western Labour Markets.* Oxford: Oxford University Press.

Heath, A., Schneider, S. L., and Butt, S., 2016. *Developing a Measure of Socio-cultural Origins for the European Social Survey.* GESIS – Leibniz-Institut für Sozialwissenschaften.

Hein, J., 1993. Refugees, Immigrants, and the State. *Annual Review of Sociology,* 19, 43–59.

Helbling, M., Bjerre, L., Römer, F., and Zobel, M., 2017. Measuring Immigration Policies: The IMPIC Database. *European Political Science,* 16 (1), 79–98.

Herda, D., 2010. How Many Immigrants? Foreign-Born Population Innumeracy in Europe. *Public Opinion Quarterly,* 74 (4), 674–695.

Hirschman, C., Alba, R., and Farley, R., 2000. The Meaning and Measurement of Race in the US Census: Glimpses into the Future. *Demography,* 37 (3), 381–393.

Hochschild, J. L., and Powell, B. M., 2008. Racial Reorganization and the United States Census 1850–1930: Mulattoes, Half-Breeds, Mixed Parentage, Hindoos, and the Mexican Race. *Studies in American Political Development,* 22 (1), 59–96.

Hochschild, J. L., Weaver, V. M., and Burch, T. R., 2012. *Creating a New Racial Order: How Immigration, Multiracialism, Genomics, and the Young Can Remake Race in America.* Princeton: Princeton University Press.

Hogg, M. A., and Ridgeway, C. L., 2003. Social Identity: Sociological and Social Psychological Perspectives. *Social Psychology Quarterly,* 66 (2), 97–100.

Hogg, M. A., and Tindale, S., eds., 2001. *Handbook of Social Psychology: Group Processes.* Oxford: Blackwell.

Hollifield, J. F., 1992. *Immigrants, Markets, and States: The Political Economy of Postwar Europe.* Cambridge, MA: Harvard University Press.

Hollifield, J. F., 2006. The Emerging Migration State. *International Migration Review,* 38 (3), 885–912.

Holmes, S. M., and Castañeda, H., 2016. Representing the "European Refugee Crisis" in Germany and Beyond: Deservingness and Difference, Life and Death. *American Ethnologist,* 43 (1), 12–24.

Hopkins, D. J., Sides, J., and Citrin, J., 2016. The Muted

Consequences of Correct Information About Immigration. *Journal of Politics*, 81 (1), 315–320.

Housen, T., Hopkins, S., and Earnest, J., 2013. A Systematic Review on the Impact of Internal Remittances on Poverty and Consumption in Developing Countries: Implications for Policy. *Population, Space and Place*, 19 (5), 610–632.

Hunt, J., 1992. The Impact of the 1962 Repatriates from Algeria on the French Labor Market. *Industrial and Labor Relations Review*, 45 (3), 556–572.

Ichou, M., 2014. Who They Were There: Immigrants' Educational Selectivity and Their Children's Educational Attainment. *European Sociological Review*, 30 (6), 750–765.

Ignatiev, N., 1995. *How the Irish Became White*. New York: Routledge.

IOM, 2017. *World Migration Report 2018*. International Organisation for Migration.

Jacobs, D., and Rea, A., 2005. Construction et importation des classements ethniques: Allochtones et immigrés aux Pays-Bas et en Belgique. *Revue Européenne des Migrations Internationales*, 21 (2), 35–59.

Jacobson, M. F., 1999. *Whiteness of a Different Color: European Immigrants and the Alchemy of Race*. Cambridge, MA: Harvard University Press.

Jamal, M. A., 2015. The "Tiering" of Citizenship and Residency and the "Hierarchization" of Migrant Communities: The United Arab Emirates in Historical Context. *International Migration Review*, 49 (3), 601–632.

Jasso, G., 2011. Migration and Stratification. *Social Science Research*, 40 (5), 1292–1336.

Jenkins, R., 1994. Rethinking Ethnicity: Identity, Categorization and Power. *Ethnic & Racial Studies*, 17 (2), 197–223.

Jenkins, R., 1997. *Rethinking Ethnicity: Arguments and Explorations*. London: Sage.

Jiménez, T. R., 2008. Mexican Immigrant Replenishment and the Continuing Significance of Ethnicity and Race. *American Journal of Sociology*, 113 (6), 1527–1567.

Jiménez, T. R., and Horowitz, A. L., 2013. When White Is Just Alright: How Immigrants Redefine Achievement and Reconfigure the Ethnoracial Hierarchy. *American Sociological Review*, 78 (5), 849–871.

Joppke, C., 1999. How Immigration Is Changing Citizenship:

A Comparative View. *Ethnic and Racial Studies*, 22 (4), 629–652.

Joppke, C., 2010. *Citizenship and Immigration*. Cambridge: Polity Press.

Joppke, C., 2017. Citizenship in Immigration States. In: *The Oxford Handbook of Citizenship*. Oxford Handbooks Online.

Joppke, C., 2019. The Instrumental Turn of Citizenship. *Journal of Ethnic and Migration Studies*, 45 (6), 858–878.

Kalantaryan, S., and Martin, I., 2015. *Reforming the EU Blue Card as a Labour Migration Policy Tool?* Migration Policy Centre, European University Institute.

Kaplan, H. S., Hill, K., and Hurtado, A. M., 2011. The Embodied Capital Theory of Human Evolution. In: Ellison, P. T., ed., *Reproductive Ecology and Human Evolution*. Hawthorne: Aldine de Gruyter, 293–318.

Kasinitz, P., 2008. Becoming American, Becoming Minority, Getting Ahead: The Role of Racial and Ethnic Status in the Upward Mobility of the Children of Immigrants. *Annals of the American Academy of Political and Social Science*, 620 (1), 253–269.

Kasinitz, P., and Vickerman, M., 2001. Ethnic Niches and Racial Traps: Jamaicans in the New York Regional Economy. In: Cordero-Guzmán, H. R., Smith, R. C., and Grosfoguel, R., eds., *Migration, Transnationalization, and Race in a Changing New York*. Philadelphia: Temple University Press, 191–211.

Kasinitz, P., Mollenkopf, J., and Waters, M. C., 2002. Becoming American/Becoming New Yorkers: Immigrant Incorporation in a Majority Minority City. *International Migration Review*, 36 (4), 1020–1036.

Kasinitz, P., Mollenkopf, J., Waters, M. C., and Holdaway, J., 2008. *Inheriting the City: The Children of Immigrants Come of Age*. New York: Russell Sage Foundation.

Kastoryano, R., 2002. *Negotiating Identities: States and Immigrants in France and Germany*. Princeton: Princeton University Press.

Kastoryano, R., 2006. Vers un nationalisme transnational. Redéfinir la nation, le nationalisme et le territoire. *Revue française de science politique*, 56 (4), 533–553.

Kim, C. J., 1999. The Racial Triangulation of Asian Americans. *Politics & Society*, 27 (1), 105–138.

Kivisto, P., 2001. Theorizing Transnational Immigration: A Critical Review of Current Efforts. *Ethnic & Racial Studies*, 24 (4), 549–577.

Kofman, E., 2002. Contemporary European Migrations, Civic Stratification and Citizenship. *Political Geography*, 21 (8), 1035–1054.

Koopmans, R., Michalowski, I., and Waibel, S., 2012. Citizenship Rights for Immigrants: National Political Processes and Cross-National Convergence in Western Europe, 1980–2008. *American Journal of Sociology*, 117 (4), 1202–1245.

Korzeniewicz, R. P., and Moran, T. P., 2009. *Unveiling Inequality: A World-Historical Perspective*. New York: Russell Sage Foundation.

Kubal, A., 2013. Conceptualizing Semi-Legality in Migration Research. *Law & Society Review*, 47 (3), 555–587.

Lakhani, S. M., 2013. Producing Immigrant Victims' "Right" to Legal Status and the Management of Legal Uncertainty. *Law & Social Inquiry*, 38 (2), 442–473.

Lakhani, S. M., and Timmermans, S., 2014. Biopolitical Citizenship in the Immigration Adjudication Process. *Social Problems*, 61 (3), 360–379.

Lamont, M., 1999. *The Cultural Territories of Race: Black and White Boundaries*. New York: Russell Sage Foundation.

Lamont, M., 2000. *The Dignity of Working Men: Morality and the Boundaries of Race, Class, and Immigration*. Cambridge, MA: Harvard University Press.

Lamont, M., 2012. Toward a Comparative Sociology of Valuation and Evaluation. *Annual Review of Sociology*, 38 (1), 201–221.

Lamont, M., and Duvoux, N., 2014. How Neo-Liberalism Has Transformed France's Symbolic Boundaries? *French Politics, Culture & Society*, 32 (2), 57–75.

Lamont, M., and Molnar, V., 2002. The Study of Boundaries in the Social Sciences. *Annual Review of Sociology*, 28, 167–195.

Lamont, M., Beljean, S., and Clair, M., 2014. What is Missing? Cultural Processes and Causal Pathways to Inequality. *Socio-Economic Review*, 12 (3), 573–608.

Le Renard, A., 2019. *Le Privilège occidental: Travail, intimité et hiérarchies postcoloniales à Dubaï*. Paris: Presses de Sciences Po.

Lee, E. S., 1966. A Theory of Migration. *Demography*, 3 (1), 47–57.

Lee, J., and Bean, F. D., 2004. America's Changing Color Lines: Immigration, Race/Ethnicity, and Multiracial Identification. *Annual Review of Sociology*, 30, 221–242.

Lee, S. K., 2017. The Three Worlds of Emigration Policy: Towards a Theory of Sending State Regimes. *Journal of Ethnic and Migration Studies*, 43 (9), 1453–1471.

Lee, T. L., and Fiske, S. T., 2012. Xenophobia and How to Fight It: Immigrants as the Quintessential 'Other'. *In*: Wiley, S., Philogene, G., and Revenson, T., eds., *Social Categories in Everyday Experience*. Washington, DC: American Psychological Association, 151–163.

Lentin, A., 2016. Eliminating Race Obscures its Trace: Theories of Race and Ethnicity Symposium. *Ethnic and Racial Studies*, 39 (3), 383–391.

Leonardo, M. D., 1984. *The Varieties of Ethnic Experience: Kinship, Class, and Gender among California Italian-Americans*. Ithaca: Cornell University Press.

Lersch, P. M., 2015. Family Migration and Subsequent Employment: The Effect of Gender Ideology. *Journal of Marriage and Family*, 78 (1), 230–245.

Levitt, P., 2001. *The Transnational Villagers*. Berkeley: University of California Press.

Levitt, P., 2003. "You Know, Abraham Was Really the First Immigrant": Religion and Transnational Migration. *International Migration Review*, 37 (3), 847–873.

Levitt, P., and de la Dehesa, R., 2010. Transnational Migration and the Redefinition of the State: Variations and Explanations. *Ethnic and Racial Studies*, 26 (4), 587–611.

Levitt, P., and Jaworsky, B. N., 2007. Transnational Migration Studies: Past Developments and Future Trends. *Annual Review of Sociology*, 33 (1), 129–156.

Levitt, P., and Schiller, N. G., 2004. Conceptualizing Simultaneity: A Transnational Social Field Perspective on Society. *International Migration Review*, 38 (3), 1002–1039.

Lichter, D. T., 2013. Integration or Fragmentation? Racial Diversity and the American Future. *Demography*, 50 (2), 359–391.

Lieberson, S., 1981. *A Piece of the Pie: Blacks and White Immigrants since 1880*. Berkeley: University of California Press.

Liebig, T., and Sousa-Poza, A., 2004. Migration, Self-Selection and Income Inequality: An International Analysis. *Kyklos*, 57 (1), 125–146.

Liebler, C. A., Porter, S. R., Fernandez, L. E., Noon, J. M., and Ennis, S. R., 2017. America's Churning Races: Race and Ethnicity Response Changes Between Census 2000 and the 2010 Census. *Demography*, 54 (1), 259–284.

Light, M. T., Massoglia, M., and King, R. D., 2014. Citizenship and Punishment: The Salience of National Membership in U.S. Criminal Courts. *American Sociological Review*, 79 (5), 825–847.

Lin, K.-H., and Weiss, I., 2019. Immigration and Wage Distribution in the United States. *Demography*, forthcoming.

Lochak, D., 2013. Qu'est-ce qu'un réfugié ? La construction politique d'une catégorie juridique. *Pouvoirs*, 144 (1), 33–47.

Loewen, J. W., 1971. *The Mississippi Chinese: Between Black and White*. Cambridge, MA: Harvard University Press.

Long, K., 2013. When Refugees Stopped Being Migrants: Movement, Labour and Humanitarian Protection. *Migration Studies*, 1 (1), 4–26.

Long, K., 2014. *The Huddled Masses: Immigration and Inequality*. London: Thistle Publishing.

Longhi, S., Nijkamp, P., and Poot, J., 2005. A Meta-Analytic Assessment of the Effect of Immigration on Wages. *Journal of Economic Surveys*, 19 (3), 451–477.

Longhi, S., Nijkamp, P., and Poot, J., 2010. Joint Impacts of Immigration on Wages and Employment: Review and Meta-Analysis. *Journal of Geographical Systems*, 12 (4), 355–387.

Longva, A. N., 1999. Keeping Migrant Workers in Check: The Kafala System in the Gulf. *Middle East Report*, (211), 20–22.

Lorcerie, F., 2007. Le Primordialisme français, ses voies, ses fièvres. *In*: Smouts, M.-C., ed., *La Situation postcoloniale. Les Postcolonial Studies dans le débat français*. Paris: Presses de Sciences Po, 298–343.

Lorcerie, F., ed., 2010. *Pratiquer les frontières. Jeunes migrants et descendants de migrants dans l'espace franco-maghrébin*. Paris: Centre National de la Recherche Scientifique.

Lowell, B. L., and Avato, J., 2014. The Wages of Skilled Temporary Migrants: Effects of Visa Pathways and Job Portability. *International Migration*, 52 (3), 85–98.

Lucassen, J., and Lucassen, L., 2017. Theorizing Cross-Cultural Migrations: The Case of Eurasia since 1500. *Social Science History*, 41 (3), 445–475.

Lucassen, L., and Lucassen, J., 2014. Quantifying and Qualifying Cross-Cultural Migrations in Europe since 1500: A Plea for a Broader View. *In*: Fauri, F., ed., *The History of Migration in Europe: Perspectives from Economics, Politics and Sociology*. New York: Routledge, 13–38.

Luthra, R., Waldinger, R., and Soehl, T., 2018. *Origins and Destinations: The Making of the Second Generation*. New York: Russell Sage Foundation.

Lyman, S. M., and Douglass, W. A., 1973. Ethnicity: Strategies of Collective and Individual Impression Management. *Social Research*, 40 (2), 344–355.

Mangum, C. S., 1940. *The Legal Status of the Negro*. Chapel Hill: University of North Carolina Press.

Manning, P., 2013. *Migration in World History*. New York: Routledge.

Manza, J., and Sauder, M., eds., 2009. *Inequality and Society. Social Perspectives on Social Stratification*. New York: W.W. Norton & Company.

Marrow, H., 2011. *New Destination Dreaming: Immigration, Race, and Legal Status in the Rural American South*. Stanford: Stanford University Press.

Marshall, T. H., 1950. *Citizenship and Social Class*. Cambridge: Cambridge University Press.

Marshall, T. H., 1964. *Class, Citizenship and Soical Development: Essays*. New York: Doubleday.

Martín, D. C., 2008. Rules, Red Tape, and Paperwork: The Archaeology of State Control over Migrants. *Journal of Historical Sociology*, 21 (1), 82–119.

Martinez, O., Wu, E., Sandfort, T., Dodge, B., Carballo-Dieguez, A., Pinto, R., Rhodes, S., Moya, E., and Chavez-Baray, S., 2015. Evaluating the Impact of Immigration Policies on Health Status Among Undocumented Immigrants: A Systematic Review, 17 (3), 947–970.

Martiniello, M., and Simon, P., 2005. Les enjeux de la catégorisation. *Revue Européenne des Migrations Internationales*, 21 (2), 7–18.

Martín-Pérez, A., and Moreno-Fuentes, F. J., 2012. Migration and Citizenship Law in Spain: Path-dependency and Policy

Change in a Recent Country of Immigration. *International Migration Review*, 46 (3), 625–655.

Marx, K., 1976. *Capital, Volume 1*. London: Penguin.

Massey, D. S., 1995. The New Immigration and Ethnicity in the United States. *Population and Development Review*, 21 (3), 631–652.

Massey, D. S., 1999. Why does Immigration Occur? A Theoretical Synthesis. *In*: Hirschman, C., Kasinitz, P., and DeWind, J., eds., *The Handbook of International Migration: The American Experience*. New York: Russel Sage Foundation, 34–52.

Massey, D. S., 2007. *Categorically Unequal. The American Stratification System*. New York: Russell Sage Foundation.

Massey, D. S., 2009. Racial Formation in Theory and Practice: The Case of Mexicans in the United States. *Race and Social Problems*, 1 (1), 12–26.

Massey, D. S., and Bartley, K., 2005. The Changing Legal Status Distribution of Immigrants: A Caution. *International Migration Review*, 39 (2), 469–484.

Massey, D. S., and Denton, N., 1993. *American Apartheid: Segregation and the Making of the Underclass*. Cambridge, MA: Harvard University Press.

Massey, D. S., and Gelatt, J., 2010. What Happened to the Wages of Mexican Immigrants? Trends and Interpretations. *Latino Studies*, 8 (3), 328–354.

Massey, D. S., and Riosmena, F., 2010. Undocumented Migration from Latin America in an Era of Rising US Enforcement. *Annals of the American Academy of Political and Social Science*, 630 (1), 294–321.

Massey, D. S., and Taylor, J. E., eds., 2004. *International Migration: Prospects and Policies in a Global Market*. Oxford: Oxford University Press.

Massey, D. S., Arango, J., Hugo, G., Kouaouci, A., Pellegrino, A., and Taylor, J. E., 1993. Theories of International Migration: A Review and Appraisal. *Population and Development Review*, 19 (3), 431–466.

Massey, D. S., Durand, J., and Malone, N. J., 2002. *Beyond Smoke and Mirrors: Mexican Immigration in an Era of Economic Integration*. New York: Russell Sage Foundation.

Matthews, G., and Ruhs, M., 2007. Are You Being Served? Employer Demand for Migrant Labour in the UK's Hospitality

Sector. Centre on Migration, Policy and Society, Working Paper 51.

Mayda, A. M., 2010. International Migration: A Panel Data Analysis of the Determinants of Bilateral Flows. *Journal of Population Economics*, 23 (4), 1249–1274.

McAvay, H., 2018. How Durable are Ethnoracial Segregation and Spatial Disadvantage? Intergenerational Contextual Mobility in France. *Demography*, 55 (4), 1507–1545.

McCall, L., 2001. *Complex Inequality: Gender, Class and Race in the New Economy*. New York: Routledge.

McCall, L., 2016. Political and Policy Responses to Problems of Inequality and Opportunity: Past, Present, and Future. *In*: Kirsch, I., and Braun, H., eds., *The Dynamics of Opportunity in America: Evidence and Perspectives*. Cham: Springer, 415–442.

McDermott, M., and Samson, F. L., 2005. White Racial and Ethnic Identity in the United States. *Annual Review of Sociology*, 31, 245–261.

McDowell, P. L., 2009. Old and New European Economic Migrants: Whiteness and Managed Migration Policies. *Journal of Ethnic and Migration Studies*, 35 (1), 19–36.

McGhee, D., Moreh, C., and Vlachantoni, A., 2017. An "Undeliberate Determinacy"? The Changing Migration Strategies of Polish Migrants in the UK in Times of Brexit. *Journal of Ethnic and Migration Studies*, 43 (13), 2109–2130.

McKenzie, D., and Rapoport, H., 2007. Network Effects and the Dynamics of Migration and Inequality: Theory and Evidence from Mexico. *Journal of Development Economics*, 84 (1), 1–24.

McTague, T., Stainback, K., and Tomaskovic-Devey, D., 2009. An Organizational Approach to Understanding Sex and Race Segregation in US Workplaces. *Social Forces*, 87 (3), 1499–1527.

Meissner, D., Kerwin, D. M., Chishti, M., and Bergeron, C., 2013. *Immigration Enforcement in the United States: The Rise of a Formidable Machinery*. Washington, DC: Migration Policy Institute.

Meissner, F., 2018. Legal Status Diversity: Regulating to Control and Everyday Contingencies. *Journal of Ethnic and Migration Studies*, 44 (2), 287–306.

Melzer, S. M., Tomaskovic-Devey, D., Schunck, R., and Jacobebbinghaus, P., 2018. A Relational Inequality Approach to First- and Second-Generation Immigrant Earnings in German Workplaces. *Social Forces*, 97 (1), 91–128.

Menjivar, C., 2006. Liminal Legality: Salvadoran and Guatemalan Immigrants' Lives in the United States. *American Journal of Sociology*, 111 (4), 999–1037.

Menjivar, C., 2014. Immigration Law Beyond Borders: Externalizing and Internalizing Border Controls in an Era of Securitization. *Annual Review of Law and Social Science*, 10 (1), 353–369.

Menjivar, C., and Abrego, L. J., 2012. Legal Violence: Immigration Law and the Lives of Central American Immigrants. *American Journal of Sociology*, 117 (5), 1380–1421.

Menjivar, C., and Lakhani, S. M., 2016. Transformative Effects of Immigration Law: Immigrants' Personal and Social Metamorphoses through Regularization. *American Journal of Sociology*, 121 (6), 1818–1855.

Merolla, J., Ramakrishnan, S. K., and Haynes, C., 2013. "Illegal," "Undocumented," or "Unauthorized": Equivalency Frames, Issue Frames, and Public Opinion on Immigration. *Perspectives on Politics*, 11 (3), 789–807.

Meyer, J. W., Boli, J., Thomas, G. M., and Ramirez, F. O., 1997. World Society and the Nation-State. *American Journal of Sociology*, 103 (1), 144–181.

Milanovic, B., 2005. *Worlds Apart: Measuring International and Global Inequality*. Princeton: Princeton University Press.

Milanovic, B., 2016. *Global Inequality: A New Approach for the Age of Globalization*. Cambridge, MA: Harvard University Press.

Miles, R., 1982. *Racism and Migrant Labour*. London: Routledge.

Miles, R., 1984. Marxism versus the Sociology of "Race Relations"? *Ethnic & Racial Studies*, 7 (2), 217.

Miles, R., 1989. *Racism*. London: Routledge.

Miles, R., 1993. *Racism after "Race Relations"*. London: Routledge.

Mills, M. B., 2003. Gender and Inequality in the Global Labor Force. *Annual Review of Anthropology*, 32 (1), 41–62.

Mincer, J., 1958. Investment in Human Capital and Personal Income Distribution. *Journal of Political Economy*, 66 (4), 281–302.

Mize, R., and Swords, A., 2010. *Consuming Mexican Labor:*

From the Bracero Program to NAFTA. Toronto: University of Toronto Press.

Modood, T., 2005. *Multicultural Politics: Racism, Ethnicity and Muslims in Britain.* Minneapolis: University of Minnesota Press.

Mongia, R., 2018. *Indian Migration and Empire: A Colonial Genealogy of the Modern State.* Durham: Duke University Press.

Mora, G. C., 2014. *Making Hispanics: How Activists, Bureaucrats, and Media Constructed a New American.* Chicago: University of Chicago Press.

Morawska, E., 2003. Immigrant Transnationalism and Assimilation: A Variety of Combinations and a Theoretical Model They Suggest. *In*: Joppke, C., and Morawska, E., eds., *Toward Assimilation and Citizenship in Liberal Nation-States.* Basingstoke: Palgrave, 133–176.

Morning, A., 2003. New Faces, Old Faces: Counting the Multiracial Population Past and Present. *In*: Winters, L. I., and DeBose, H. L., eds., *New Faces in a Changing America: Multiracial Identity in the 21st Century.* Thousand Oaks: Sage Publications, 41–67.

Morning, A., 2005. Multiracial Classification on the United States Census: Myth, Reality, and Future Impact. *Revue Européenne des Migrations Internationales*, 21 (2), 111–134.

Morris, L., 2002. *Managing Migration.* New York: Routledge.

Mosley, L., and Singer, D. A., 2015. Migration, Labor, and the International Political Economy. *Annual Review of Political Science*, 18 (1), 283–301.

Motomura, H., 2007. *Americans in Waiting: The Lost Story of Immigration and Citizenship in the United States.* Oxford, New York: Oxford University Press.

Motomura, H., 2008. *Immigration Outside the Law (Article 2008).* Social Science Research Network.

Motomura, H., 2014. *Immigration Outside the Law.* Oxford: Oxford University Press.

Neckerman, K. M., and Kirschenman, J., 1991. Hiring Strategies, Racial Bias, and Inner-City Workers. *Social Problems*, 38 (4), 433–447.

Neckerman, K. M., and Torche, F., 2007. Inequality: Causes and Consequences. *Annual Review of Sociology*, 33, 335–357.

Newton, L., 2008. *Illegal, Alien, or Immigrant: The Politics of Immigration Reform*. New York: New York University Press.

Ngozi Adichie, C., 2013. *Americanah*. New York: Alfred A. Knopf.

Nicholls, W. J., 2013. Making Undocumented Immigrants into a Legitimate Political Subject: Theoretical Observations from the United States and France. *Theory, Culture & Society*, 30 (3), 82–107.

Nijkamp, P., Poot, J., and Sahin, M., 2012. *Migration Impact Assessment: New Horizons*. Cheltenham: Edward Elgar Publishing.

Noiriel, G., 1984. *Longwy, immigrés et prolétaires 1880–1980*. Paris: Presses Universitaires de France.

Noiriel, G., 1988. *Le Creuset français, histoire de l'immigration (19ème, 20ème siècle)*. Paris: Seuil.

Noiriel, G., 2001. *État, nation et immigration: Vers une histoire du pouvoir*. Paris: Belin.

OECD, 2008. *Return Migration: A New Perspective*. Paris: OECD Publishing.

OECD, 2010. *Naturalisation: A Passport for the Better Integration of Immigrants?* Paris: OECD Publishing.

OECD, 2012. *Settling In: OECD Indicators of Immigrant Integration*. Paris: OECD Publishing.

OECD, 2017. *Catching Up? Intergenerational Mobility and Children of Immigrants*. Paris: OECD Publishing.

OECD, 2018. *International Migration Outlook*. Paris: OECD Publishing.

OECD and EU, 2016. *Recruiting Immigrant Workers: Europe 2016*. Paris: OECD Publishing.

Okamoto, D. G., 2014. *Redefining Race: Asian American Panethnicity and Shifting Ethnic Boundaries*. New York: Russell Sage Foundation.

Omi, M., and Winant, H., 1994. *Racial Formation in the United States: From the 1960s to the 1990s*. New York: Routledge.

Ortega, F., and Peri, G., 2009. The Causes and Effects of International Migrations: Evidence from OECD Countries 1980–2005. National Bureau of Economic Research, Working Paper 14833.

Ottaviano, G. I. P., and Peri, G., 2006. The Economic Value of Cultural Diversity: Evidence from US Cities. *Journal of Economic Geography*, 6 (1), 9–44.

Ottaviano, G. I. P., and Peri, G., 2008. Immigration and National Wages: Clarifying the Theory and the Empirics. National Bureau of Economic Research, Working Paper 14188.

Ottaviano, G. I. P., and Peri, G., 2012. Rethinking the Effect of Immigration on Wages. *Journal of the European Economic Association*, 10 (1), 152–197.

Özden, Ç., Parsons, C. R., Schiff, M., and Walmsley, T. L., 2011. Where on Earth is Everybody? The Evolution of Global Bilateral Migration 1960–2000. *World Bank Economic Review*, 25 (1), 12–56.

Pager, D., and Shepherd, H., 2008. The Sociology of Discrimination: Racial Discrimination in Employment, Housing, Credit, and Consumer Markets. *Annual Review of Sociology*, 34, 181–209.

Park, R. E., 1928. Human Migration and the Marginal Man. *American Journal of Sociology*, 33 (6), 881–893.

Park, R. E., and Burgess, E. W., 1921. *Introduction to the Science of Sociology*. Chicago: University of Chicago Press.

Parsons, T., 1951. *The Social System*. New York: Routledge.

Pascoe, E. A., and Smart Richman, L., 2009. Perceived Discrimination and Health: A Meta-analytic Review. *Psychological Bulletin*, 135 (4), 531.

Paul, K., 1997. *Whitewashing Britain: Race and Citizenship in the Postwar Era*. Ithaca: Cornell University Press.

Pedraza, S., 1991. Women and Migration: The Social Consequences of Gender. *Annual Review of Sociology*, 17, 303–325.

Peri, G., 2016. Immigrants, Productivity, and Labor Markets. *Journal of Economic Perspectives*, 30 (4), 3–30.

Peri, G., Shih, K., and Sparber, C., 2015. STEM Workers, H-1B Visas, and Productivity in US Cities. *Journal of Labor Economics*, 33 (S1), S225–S255.

Pessar, P. R., and Mahler, S. J., 2003. Transnational Migration: Bringing Gender In. *International Migration Review*, 37 (3), 812–846.

Phillips, J. A., and Massey, D. S., 1999. The New Labor Market: Immigrants and Wages after IRCA. *Demography*, 36 (2), 233–246.

Piché, V., 2013. Contemporary Migration Theories as Reflected in Their Founding Texts. *Population (English Edition)*, 68 (1), 141–164.

Piketty, T., 2014. *Capital in the Twenty First Century*. Cambridge, MA: Harvard University Press.

Piore, M. J., 1978. Dualism in the Labor Market: A Response to Uncertainty and Flux. The Case of France. *Revue Économique*, 29 (1), 26–48.

Piore, M. J., 1979. *Birds of Passage: Migrant Labor and Industrial Societies*. Cambridge: Cambridge University Press.

Portes, A., 1997. *Globalization from Below: The Rise of Transnational Communities*. Oxford: University of Oxford Transnational Communities Programme.

Portes, A., and Rumbaut, R. G., 2001. *Legacies. The Story of the Immigrant Second Generation*. Berkeley: University of California Press.

Portes, A., and Zhou, M., 1993. The New Second Generation: Segmented Assimilation and Its Variants. *Annals of the American Academy of Political and Social Science*, 530, 74–96.

Portes, A., Guarnizo, L. E., and Haller, W. J., 2002. Transnational Entrepreneurs: An Alternative Form of Immigrant Economic Adaptation. *American Sociological Review*, 67 (2), 278–298.

Portes, A., Guarnizo, L. E., and Landolt, P., 1999. The Study of Transnationalism: Pitfalls and Promise of an Emergent Research Field. *Ethnic and Racial Studies*, 22 (2), 217–237.

Pritchett, L., 2006. *Let Their People Come: Breaking the Gridlock on Global Labor Mobility*. Washington, DC: Center for Global Development.

Quijano, A., 2000. Coloniality of Power and Eurocentrism in Latin America. *International Sociology*, 15 (2), 215–232.

Quillian, L., 2008. Does Unconscious Racism Exist? *Social Psychology Quarterly*, 71 (1), 6–11.

Quillian, L., Pager, D., Hexel, O., and Midtbøen, A. H., 2017. Meta-analysis of Field Experiments Shows No Change in Racial Discrimination in Hiring Over Time. *Proceedings of the National Academy of Sciences*, 114 (41), 10870–10875.

Rathelot, R., and Safi, M., 2013. Local Ethnic Composition and Natives' and Immigrants' Geographic Mobility in France (1982–1999). *American Sociological Review*, 79 (1), 43–64.

Ravenstein, E. G., 1885. The Laws of Migration. *Journal of the Statistical Society of London*, 48 (2), 167–235.

Ravenstein, E. G., 1889. The Laws of Migration. *Journal of the Royal Statistical Society*, 52 (2), 241–305.

Rawls, J., 1971. *A Theory of Justice*. Cambridge, MA: Harvard University Press.

Rea, A., 2013. Les nouvelles figures du travailleur immigré: Fragmentation des statuts d'emploi et européanisation des migrations. *Revue Européenne des Migrations Internationales*, Vol. 29 (2), 15–35.

Recchi, E., 2015. *Mobile Europe. The Theory and Practices of Free Movement in the EU*. Basingstoke: Palgrave Macmillan.

Recchi, E., 2016. The Citizenship Gap in European Societies: Conceptualizing, Measuring and Comparing "Migration Neutrality" across the EU. *International Migration*, 54 (6), 181–200.

Recchi, E., Deutschmann, E., and Vespe, M., 2019. *Estimating Transnational Human Mobility on a Global scale*. Working Paper.

Reskin, B. F., 2003. Including Mechanisms in Our Models of Ascriptive Inequality: 2002 Presidential Address. *American Sociological Review*, 68 (1), 1–21.

Richmond, A. H., 1956. Immigration as a Social Process: The Case of Coloured Colonials in the United Kingdom. *Social and Economic Studies*, 5 (2), 185–201.

Richmond, A. H., 1978. Migration, Ethnicity and Race Relations. *Ethnic & Racial Studies*, 1 (1), 1–18.

Ridgeway, C. L., 2001. Social Status and Group Structure. *In*: Hogg, M. A., and Tindale, S., eds., *Handbook of Social Psychology: Group Processes*. Malden: Wiley-Blackwell, 352–375.

Ridgeway, C. L., 2011. *Framed by Gender: How Gender Inequality Persists in the Modern World*. New York: Oxford University Press.

Ridgeway, C. L., 2014. Why Status Matters for Inequality. *American Sociological Review*, 79 (1), 1–16.

Ridgeway, C. L., and Balkwell, J. W., 1997. Group Processes and the Diffusion of Status Beliefs. *Social Psychology Quarterly*, 60 (1), 14–31.

Ridgeway, C. L., and Correll, S. J., 2000. Limiting Inequality through Interaction: The End(s) of Gender. *Contemporary Sociology*, 29 (1), 110–120.

Ridgeway, C. L., and Correll, S. J., 2006. Consensus and the Creation of Status Beliefs. *Social Forces*, 85 (1), 431–453.

Ridgeway, C. L., and Kricheli-Katz, T., 2013. Intersecting Cultural Beliefs in Social Relations: Gender, Race, and Class Binds and Freedoms. *Gender and Society*, 27 (3), 294–318.

Rodriguez, C., 2000. *Changing Race: Latinos, the Census and the History of Ethnicity in the United States*. New York: New York University Press.

Roediger, D. R., 2005. *Working toward Whiteness. How America's Immigrants Became White*. New York: Basic Books.

Rosenblum, M. R., and Meissner, D., 2014. *The Deportation Dilemma: Reconciling Tough and Humane Enforcement*. Washington, DC: Migration Policy Institute.

Roth, W. D., 2009. "Latino Before the World": The Transnational Extension of Panethnicity. *Ethnic and Racial Studies*, 32 (6), 927–947.

Roth, W. D., 2012. *Race Migrations: Latinos and the Cultural Transformation of Race*. Stanford: Stanford University Press.

Roth, W. D., 2016. The Multiple Dimensions of Race. *Ethnic and Racial Studies*, 39 (8), 1310–1338.

Roth, W. D., and Kim, N. Y., 2013. Relocating Prejudice: A Transnational Approach to Understanding Immigrants' Racial Attitudes. *International Migration Review*, 47 (2), 330–373.

Ruhs, M., 2017. The Impact of Acquiring EU Status on the Earnings of East European Migrants in the UK: Evidence from a Quasi-Natural Experiment. *British Journal of Industrial Relations*, 55 (4), 716–750.

Ruhs, M., and Anderson, B., 2012. *Who Needs Migrant Workers? Labour Shortages, Immigration, and Public Policy*. Oxford: Oxford University Press.

Rumbaut, R. G., 1994. The Crucible Within: Ethnic Identity, Self-Esteem, and Segmented Assimilation among Children of Immigrants. *International Migration Review*, 28 (4), 748–794.

Rumbaut, R. G., 2004. Ages, Life Stages, and Generational Cohorts: Decomposing the Immigrant First and Second Generations in the United States. *International Migration Review*, 38 (3), 1160–1205.

Sadiq, K., 2008. *Paper Citizens: How Illegal Immigrants Acquire Citizenship in Developing Countries* [online]. Oxford: Oxford University Press. Available from: http://

www.oxfordscholarship.com/view/10.1093/acprof:oso/
9780195371222.001.0001/acprof-9780195371222.

Safi, M., 2010. Immigrants' Life Satisfaction in Europe: Between Assimilation and Discrimination. *European Sociological Review*, 26 (2), 159–176.

Safi, M., 2014. *Shifting Focus: Policies to Support the Labor Market Integration of New Immigrants in France*. Washington, DC: Migration Policy Institute and International Labour Office.

Safi, M., 2018. Varieties of Transnationalism and Its Changing Determinants across Immigrant Generations: Evidence from French Data1. *International Migration Review*, 52 (3), 853–897.

Said, E., 1978. *Orientalism*. New York: Pantheon Books.

Samuelson, P. A., 1948. International Trade and the Equalisation of Factor Prices. *Economic Journal*, 58 (230), 163–184.

Saperstein, A., and Penner, A. M., 2012. Racial Fluidity and Inequality in the United States. *American Journal of Sociology*, 118 (3), 676–727.

Saperstein, A., Penner, A. M., and Light, R., 2013. Racial Formation in Perspective: Connecting Individuals, Institutions, and Power Relations. *Annual Review of Sociology*, 39 (1), 359–378.

Sassen, S., 1988. *The Mobility of Labor and Capital: A Study in International Investment and Labor Flow*. Cambridge: Cambridge University Press.

Sassen, S., 2008. Two Stops in Today's New Global Geographies: Shaping Novel Labor Supplies and Employment Regimes. *American Behavioral Scientist*, 52 (3), 457–496.

Sayad, A., 1993. Naturels et Naturalisés. *Actes de la Recherche en Sciences Sociales*, 99, 26–35.

Sayad, A., 1994. Le mode de génération des générations "immigrées." *L'Homme et la Société*, 111 (1), 155–174.

Sayad, A., 1999. Immigration et "pensée d'État." *Actes de la Recherche en Sciences Sociales*, 129, 50–56.

Schmitt, M. T., Branscombe, N. R., Postmes, T., and Garcia, A., 2014. The Consequences of Perceived Discrimination for Psychological Well-being: A Meta-Analytic Review. *Psychological Bulletin*, 140 (4), 921.

Schmoll, C., and Tahir, N. B., eds., 2018. *Méditerranée: Des frontières à la dérive.* Paris: École des Hautes Études en Sciences Sociales.

Schor, P., 2017. *Counting Americans: How the US Census Classified the Nation.* New York: Oxford University Press.

Scott, J. C., 1976. *The Moral Economy of the Peasant: Rebellion and Subsistence in Southeast Asia.* New Haven: Yale University Press.

Sejersen, T. B., 2008. "I Vow to Thee My Countries": The Expansion of Dual Citizenship in the 21st Century. *The International Migration Review*, 42 (3), 523–549.

Sen, A. K., 1979. Equality of What? *In*: McMurrin, S., ed., *Tanner Lectures on Human Values.* Cambridge: Cambridge University Press, 195–220.

Sen, A. K., 2009. *The Idea of Justice.* Cambridge, MA: Harvard University Press.

Shachar, A., 2009. *The Birthright Lottery: Citizenship and Global Inequality.* Cambridge, MA: Harvard University Press.

Sharkey, P., 2013. *Stuck in Place: Urban Neighborhoods and the End of Progress toward Racial Equality.* Chicago: University of Chicago Press.

Shibutani, T., and Kwan, K. M., 1965. *Ethnic Stratification: A Comparative Approach.* New York: Macmillan.

Sides, J. 2016., 2016. Stories or Science? Facts, Frames, and Policy Attitudes. *American Politics Research*, 44 (3), 387–414.

Sides, J., and Citrin, J., 2007. European Opinion About Immigration: The Role of Identities, Interests and Information. *British Journal of Political Science*, 37 (3), 477–504.

Sigona, N., and Trehan, N., 2009. *Romani Politics in Contemporary Europe: Poverty, Ethnic Mobilization, and the Neoliberal Order.* New York: Palgrave Macmillan.

Silverstein, P. A., 2005. Immigrant Racialization and the New Savage Slot: Race, Migration, and Immigration in the New Europe. *Annual Review of Anthropology*, 34 (1), 363–384.

Simon, P., 2008. The Choice of Ignorance: The Debate on Ethnic and Racial Statistics in France. *French Politics, Culture & Society*, 26 (1), 7–31.

Simon, P., 2012. Collecting Ethnic Statistics in Europe: A Review. *Ethnic and Racial Studies*, 35 (8), 1366–1391.

Simon, P., 2017. The Failure of the Importation of Ethno-Racial Statistics in Europe: Debates and Controversies. *Ethnic and Racial Studies*, 40 (13), 2326–2332.

Simon, P., and Escafré-Dublet, A., 2009. Représenter la diversité en politique: Une reformulation de la dialectique de la différence et de l'égalité par la doxa républicaine. *Raisons Politiques*, 35 (3), 125–141.

Simon, P., Piché, V., and Gagnon, A. A., 2015. *Social Statistics and Ethnic Diversity: Cross-National Perspectives in Classifications and Identity Politics*. New York: Springer.

Sjaastad, L. A., 1962. The Costs and Returns of Human Migration. *Journal of Political Economy*, 70 (5), 80–93.

Skeldon, R., 2000. Trends in International Migration in the Asian and Pacific Region. *International Social Science Journal*, 52 (165), 369–382.

Slack, J., 2019. *Deported to Death: How Drug Violence Is Changing Migration on the US–Mexico Border*. Berkeley: University of California Press.

Small, M. L., Harding, D. J., and Lamont, M., 2010. Reconsidering Culture and Poverty. *Annals of the American Academy of Political and Social Science*, 629 (1), 6–27.

Smith, R. C., 2005a. Racialization and Mexicans in New York. *In*: Zuniga, V., and Hernandez-Leon, R., eds., *New Destinations: Mexican Immigrants in the United States*. New York: Russell Sage Foundation, 220–243.

Smith, R. C., 2005b. *Mexican New York: The Transnational Lives of New Immigrants*. Berkeley: University of California Press.

Smith, R. C., 2014. Black Mexicans, Conjunctural Ethnicity, and Operating Identities: Long-Term Ethnographic Analysis. *American Sociological Review*, 79 (3), 517–548.

Solomos, J., and Wrench, J., 1995. *Racism and Migration in Western Europe*. Oxford: Berg Publishers.

Sorenson, A. B., 2000. Toward a Sounder Basis for Class Analysis. *American Journal of Sociology*, 105 (6), 1523–1558.

Sorokin, P. A., 1927. *Social Mobility*. New York: Harper & Row.

Soysal, Y. N., 1994. *Limits of Citizenship: Migrants and Postnational Membership in Europe*. Chicago: University of Chicago Press.

Stark, O., 1991. *The Migration of Labor*. Oxford: Blackwell.

Stark, O., 2006. Inequality and Migration: A Behavioral Link. *Economics Letters*, 91 (1), 146–152.

Stark, O., and Bloom, D. E., 1985. The New Economics

of Labor Migration. *American Economic Review*, 75 (2), 173–178.

Steel, Z., Momartin, S., Silove, D., Coello, M., Aroche, J., and Tay, K. W., 2011. Two-Year Psychosocial and Mental Health Outcomes for Refugees Subjected to Restrictive or Supportive Immigration Policies. *Social Science & Medicine*, 72 (7), 1149–1156.

Steinhardt, M. F., 2012. Does Citizenship Matter? The Economic Impact of Naturalizations in Germany. *Labour Economics*, 19 (6), 813–823.

Street, A., Jones-Correa, M., and Zepeda-Millán, C., 2017. Political Effects of Having Undocumented Parents. *Political Research Quarterly*, 70 (4), 818–832.

Stuart, F., Armenta, A., and Osborne, M., 2015. Legal Control of Marginal Groups. *Annual Review of Law and Social Science*, 11 (1), 235–254.

Tajfel, H., 1981. *Human Groups and Social Categories*. Cambridge: Cambridge University Press.

Tajfel, H., and Turner, J., 1986. The Social Identity Theory of Intergroup Behavior. *In*: Worchel, S., and Austin, W., eds., *Psychology of Intergroup Relations*. Chicago: Nelson-Hall, 7–24.

Tehranian, J., 2010. *Whitewashed: America's Invisible Middle Eastern Minority*. New York: New York University Press.

Telles, E. E., and Ortiz, V., 2008. *Generations of Exclusion: Mexican Americans, Assimilation and Race*. New York: Russel Sage Foundation.

Therborn, G., 2013. *The Killing Fields of Inequality*. Cambridge: Polity.

Thiollet, H., 2011. Migration as Diplomacy: Labor Migrants, Refugees, and Arab Regional Politics in the Oil-Rich Countries. *International Labor and Working Class History*, 79, 103–121.

Thompson, E. P., 1971. The Moral Economy of the English Crowd in the Eighteenth Century. *Past & Present*, 50, 76–136.

Tilly, C., 1998. *Durable Inequality*. Berkeley: University of California Press.

Tilly, C., 2001a. Relational origins of inequality. *Anthropological Theory*, 1 (3), 355–372.

Tilly, C., 2001b. Mechanisms in Political Processes. *Annual Review of Political Science*, 4 (1), 21–41.

Tilly, C., 2002. *Stories, Identities and Political Change*. Lanham: Rowman & Littlefield Publishers.

Tilly, C., 2003. Changing Forms of Inequality. *Sociological Theory*, 21 (1), 31–36.

Tilly, C., 2005. Historical Perspectives on Inequality. *In*: Romero, M., and Margolis, E., eds., *The Blackwell Companion to Social Inequalities*. Malden: Blackwell Publishing, 15–30.

Tomaskovic-Devey, D., 1993. *Gender and Racial Inequality at Work*. New York: Oxford University Press.

Tomaskovic-Devey, D., 2014. The Relational Generation of Workplace Inequalities. *Social Currents*, 1 (1), 51–73.

Tomaskovic-Devey, D., and Avent-Holt, D., 2019. *Relational Inequalities: An Organizational Approach*. Oxford: Oxford University Press.

Tomaskovic-Devey, D., Hällsten, M., and Avent-Holt, D., 2015. Where Do Immigrants Fare Worse? Modeling Workplace Wage Gap Variation with Longitudinal Employer–Employee Data. *American Journal of Sociology*, 120 (4), 1095–1143.

Tomaskovic-Devey, D., Stainback, K., Taylor, T., Zimmer, C., Robinson, C., and McTague, T., 2006. Documenting Desegregation: Segregation in American Workplaces by Race, Ethnicity, and Sex, 1966–2003. *American Sociological Review*, 71 (4), 565–588.

Torpey, J., 1999. *The Invention of the Passport: Surveillance, Citizenship and the State*. Cambridge: Cambridge University Press.

Torres, J. M., and Waldinger, R. D., 2015. Civic Stratification and the Exclusion of Undocumented Immigrants from Cross-Border Health Care. *Journal of Health and Social Behavior*, 56 (4), 438–459.

Triandafyllidou, A., and Isaakyan, I., 2014. *EU Management of High Skill Migration*. Florence: Robert Schuman Centre for Advanced Studies Global Governance Programme Policy Briefs.

Tyler, I., and Marciniak, K., 2013. Immigrant Protest: An Introduction. *Citizenship Studies*, 17 (2), 143–156.

UNHCR, 2017. *Global Trends: Forced Displacement in 2016*. Geneva: UNHCR.

UNHCR, 2018. *Global Trends: Forced Displacement In 2017*. Geneva: UNHCR.

Valfort, M.-A., 2017. La religion, facteur de discrimination à l'embauche en France ? *Revue Économique*, 68 (5), 895–907.

Vertovec, S., 1999. Conceiving and Researching Transnationalism. *Ethnic and Racial Studies*, 22 (2), 447–462.

Vertovec, S., 2011. The Cultural Politics of Nation and Migration. *Annual Review of Anthropology*, 40, 241–256.

Vetters, L., 2017. Migration and the Transformation of German Administrative Law: An Interdisciplinary Research Agenda. Max-Planck-Institut für ethnologische Forschung, Working Paper 188.

Vickstrom, E. R., 2014. Pathways into Irregular Status Among Senegalese Migrants in Europe. *International Migration Review*, 48 (4), 1062–1099.

Vickstrom, E. R., and González-Ferrer, A., 2016. Legal Status, Gender, and Labor Market Participation of Senegalese Migrants in France, Italy, and Spain. *Annals of the American Academy of Political and Social Science*, 666 (1), 164–202.

Violante, G. L., Durlauf, S., and Blume, L., 2016. Skill-Biased Technical Change. In: *The New Palgrave Dictionary of Economics*. New York: Springer.

Viruell-Fuentes, E. A., Miranda, P. Y., and Abdulrahim, S., 2012. More than Culture: Structural Racism, Intersectionality Theory, and Immigrant Health. *Social Science & Medicine*, 75 (12), 2099–2106.

Voss, K., and Bloemraad, I., eds., 2011. *Rallying for Immigrant Rights. The Fight for Inclusion in 21st Century America*. Berkeley: University of California Press.

Wacquant, L., 1997. For an Analytic of Racial Domination. *Political Power and Social Theory*, 11, 221–234.

Waldinger, R. D., 1995. The "Other Side" of Embeddedness: A Case Study of the Interplay of Economy and Ethnicity. *Ethnic and Racial Studies*, 18 (3), 555–580.

Waldinger, R. D., 1996. *Still the Promised City? African-Americans and New Immigrants in Postindustrial New York*. Cambridge, MA: Harvard University Press.

Waldinger, R. D., 2003. Foreigners Transformed: International Migration and the Remaking of a Divided People. *Diaspora: A Journal of Transnational Studies*, 12 (2), 247–272.

Waldinger, R. D., 2014. The Politics of Cross-border Engagement: Mexican Emigrants and the Mexican State. *Theory and Society*, 43 (5), 483–511.

Waldinger, R. D., 2015. *The Cross-Border Connection: Immigrants, Emigrants, and Their Homelands.* Cambridge, MA: Harvard University Press.

Waldinger, R. D., and Lichter, M. I., 2003. *How the Other Half Works: Immigration and the Social Organization of Labor.* Berkeley: University of California Press.

Wallerstein, I., 1974. The Rise and Future Demise of the World Capitalist System: Concepts for Comparative Analysis. *Comparative Studies in Society and History,* 16 (4), 387–415.

Wallerstein, I., 1984. *The Politics of the World Economy: The States, the Movements, and the Civilizations.* Cambridge: Cambridge University Press.

Wallerstein, I., and Balibar, É., 2007. *Race, Nation, Class.* Paris: La Découverte.

Ward, J., 2008. White Normativity: The Cultural Dimensions of Whiteness in a Racially Diverse LGBT Organization. *Sociological Perspectives,* 51 (3), 563–586.

Waters, M. C. 1990. *Ethnic Options: Choosing Identities in America.* Berkeley: University of California Press.

Waters, M. C., 1999. *Black Identities: West Indian Immigrant Dreams and American Realities.* Cambridge, MA: Harvard University Press.

Waters, M. C., and Jiménez, T., 2005. Assessing Immigrant Assimilation: New Empirical and Theoretical Challenges. *Annual Review of Sociology,* 31, 105–125.

Weber, M., 1921. *Économie et Société.* Paris: Pocket.

Western, B., 2006. *Punishment and Inequality in America.* New York: Russell Sage Foundation.

Western, B., and Pettit, B., 2010. Incarceration and Social Inequality. *Daedalus,* 139 (3), 8–19.

Wihtol de Wenden, C., 2010. *La Question migratoire au XXIe siècle. Migrants, réfugiés et relations internationales.* Paris: Presses de Sciences Po.

Wilkins, C. L., Kaiser, C. R., and Rieck, H., 2010. Detecting Racial Identification: The Role of Phenotypic Prototypicality. *Journal of Experimental Social Psychology,* 46 (6), 1029–1034.

Wilkinson, R. G., 2005. *The Impact of Inequality: How to Make Sick Societies Healthier.* London: Routledge.

Williams, E., 1944. *Capitalism and Slavery*. London: André Deutsch.

Wimmer, A., 2008. The Making and Unmaking of Ethnic Boundaries: A Multilevel Process Theory. *The American Journal of Sociology*, 113 (4), 970–1022.

Wimmer, A., 2013. *Ethnic Boundary Making: Institutions, Power, Networks*. New York: Oxford University Press.

Wimmer, A., and Min, B., 2006. From Empire to Nation-State: Explaining Wars in the Modern World, 1816–2001. *American Sociological Review*, 71 (6), 867–897.

Wimmer, A., and Schiller, N. G., 2003. Methodological Nationalism, the Social Sciences, and the Study of Migration: An Essay in Historical Epistemology. *International Migration Review*, 37 (3), 576–610.

Winant, H., 2000. Race and Race Theory. *Annual Review of Sociology*, 26, 169–185.

Winant, H., 2001. *The World is a Ghetto: Race and Democracy since World War II*. New York: Basic Books.

Winant, H., 2004. *The New Politics of Race*. Minneapolis: University of Minnesota Press.

Wong, T. K., 2015. *Rights, Deportation, and Detention in the Age of Immigration Control*. Stanford: Stanford University Press.

World Bank, 2016. *Migration and Remittances Factbook 2016*. Washington, DC: World Bank.

Wrench, J., Rea, A., and Ouali, N., 1999. *Migrants, Ethnic Minorities and the Labour Market. Integration and Exclusion in Europe*. London: Macmillan.

Wright, E. O., 1997. *Class Counts: Comparative Studies in Class Analysis*. Cambridge: Cambridge University Press.

Xu, J., and Lee, J. C., 2013. The Marginalized "Model" Minority: An Empirical Examination of the Racial Triangulation of Asian Americans. *Social Forces*, 91 (4), 1363–1397.

Yancey, G., 2003. *Who Is White? Latinos, Asians, and the New Black/Nonblack Divide*. Boulder: Lynne Rienner Publishers.

Yıldız, C., and De Genova, N. P., 2018. Un/Free Mobility: Roma Migrants in the European Union. *Social Identities*, 24 (4), 425–441.

Yoo, G. J., 2008. Immigrants and Welfare: Policy Constructions of Deservingness. *Journal of Immigrant & Refugee Studies*, 6 (4), 490–507.

Young, I. M., 2000. *Inclusion and Democracy*. Oxford: Oxford University Press.

Yuval-Davis, N., 1997. *Gender and Nation*. London: Sage Publications.

Zamora, S., 2016. Racial Remittances: The Effect of Migration on Racial Ideologies in Mexico and the United States. *Sociology of Race and Ethnicity*, 2 (4), 466–481.

Zetter, R., 2007. More Labels, Fewer Refugees: Remaking the Refugee Label in an Era of Globalization. *Journal of Refugee Studies*, 20 (2), 172–192.

Zhou, M., 1997. Segmented Assimilation: Issues, Controversies, and Recent Research on the New Second Generation. *International Migration Review*, 31 (4), 975–1008.

Zhou, M., 2009. *Contemporary Chinese America: Immigration, Ethnicity and Community Transformation*. Philadelphia: Temple University Press.

Zolberg, A. R., 2008. *A Nation by Design: Immigration Policy in the Fashioning of America*. Cambridge, MA: Harvard University Press.

Zolberg, A. R., and Woon, L. L., 1999. Why Islam is like Spanish: Cultural Incorporation in Europe and the United States. *Politics & Society*, 27 (1), 5–38.

Zolberg, A. R., Suhrke, A., and Aguayo, S., 1986. International Factors in the Formation of Refugee Movements. *International Migration Review*, 20 (2), 151–169.

Index